CW01656706

BÉA
J'espère que cette lecture te plaira !
Séverine Dalla

Séverine Dalla

C'EST DANS L'AIR !

À ceux qui pensent que les fleurs de l'avenir
sont dans toutes les graines, même minuscules, que l'on sème aujourd'hui...

Pierre a envie de prendre l'AIR.
Avec son père, il sort de la petite ville.

Rapidement, ils s'éloignent
de cette ATMOSPHERE assez singulière...

C'est parti pour une balade à pied en direction du bois, en passant devant de jolis endroits.

Ils connaissent bien Monsieur Jo, qui entretient soigneusement et sans aucun produit son potager Bio.

Il est en train de travailler son COMPOST.
Monsieur Jo fait parfois des discours ennuyeux sur la nature, le CLIMAT...

... sur le temps qu'il fait, tout ça. Mais il est quand même rigolo.
Et Pierre adore ses haricots !

« C'est fou comme on peut obtenir un bon engrais, juste en mélangeant quelques **DECHETS** ! »

« Et ça ne sent pas trop mauvais. Je vous le promets ! »

Allez, zou ! Quelques gorgées d'EAU et ils repartent.
« La boisson, toujours dans une gourde ! »

C'est Maman qui dit ça. Et puis aussi :
« Les bouteilles en plastique, c'est pas terrible pour l'ENVIRONNEMENT ! »

Ils arrivent dans la forêt. Il fait bon, il fait frais ! Entre deux jeux, la **FAUNE** et la **FLORE** sont détaillées.

Hop ! L'appareil sort du sac :
Pierre aime tout photographier.

Flore, c'est justement le prénom de sa meilleure amie, qui adore regarder ses images. Elle, son truc, c'est plutôt la récup' pour éviter le **GASPILLAGE**.

Un jour, ils ont fabriqué un cerf-volant.
C'était trop marrant !

Récemment, Flore a fabriqué un abri pour les insectes : leur **HABITAT** naturel a parfois disparu...

« Oh, peut-être un **HERISSON** ? Où a-t-il couru ? »
Pierre et son papa ont vu des traces...

Les parfums de la forêt leur chatouillent les narines.
Ici, peu d'**INDUSTRIES**, on n'est pas dérangés par les odeurs ou les fumées.

Et sans **INSECTICIDES**, de nombreuses espèces s'en donnent à cœur joie dans les sous-bois.

Ils ne trouvent pas le hérisson recherché... « Pas plus que de JAGUAR ou de KOALA, d'autres animaux menacés ! » dit Papa, un peu moqueur.

Par terre, parmi d'autres choses, des mouchoirs JETABLES. À ramasser ! Et hop, dans la première poubelle qu'on trouvera.

« Dis, tu crois qu'il peut y avoir des LOUPS chez nous ? »
Pierre en entend beaucoup parler à la télé...

« Non, ils sont encore rares. Et nous ne sommes pas sur leurs territoires !
Si près du LITTORAL nous vivons dans une région qu'ils ne visitent pas. »

Par ici, il y a quand même des espèces particulières : présents toute l'année ou **MIGRATEURS**, des poissons et des oiseaux à observer !

« Clic ! Clic ! »

Eux aussi, c'est un vrai bonheur pour Pierre de les photographier.

La maîtresse en a parlé en classe, c'était passionnant.
Elle a aussi décrit ce qui pouvait être NOCIF pour les eaux et leurs habitants.

En plus des rivières et des mares, il y a sous la terre
les NAPPES PHREATIQUES : des réserves bien utiles, mais fragiles !

Sans compter les **OCÉANS**, parfois salis par les marées noires, les rejets des usines, les **ORDURES** ménagères que nous y jetons...

Vraiment,
pauvres poissons !

Pierre, Flore et quelques amis ont décidé cette année de créer le « gang des Mains Vertes » : aidés par les grands, ils traquent les POLLUTIONS.

Depuis plusieurs mois, leur chasse est ouverte.
De petites choses, certes...

... mais ces gestes embellissent le **QUOTIDIEN**.
Et au moins, sur les photos de Pierre, il y a moins de tri à faire !

Dans la petite ville, la **QUALITE DE VIE** s'est doucement améliorée.
Papa, Maman et même Monsieur Jo les ont déjà félicités.

De nouvelles plantes sont apparues, et ce n'est pas dû au **RECHAUFFEMENT DE LA PLANETE**. Portées par le vent, des graines se sont posées...

... Et les petites pousses, personne ne les a éliminées. C'est bien agréable à regarder !

Dans la région, pas de SECHERESSE.
On a rarement besoin d'arroser.

D'ailleurs, Papa en a fait les frais : au milieu du chemin, une flaque qu'il n'avait pas vue. Et plouf ! Il a un pied trempé.

Pierre s'est retenu de rigoler. Ce petit accident sonne l'heure du goûter. Il fait attention à ne rien salir et ses restes subiront le **TRI SÉLECTIF**.

Tiens ! D'autres habitants de notre bonne vieille **TERRE** se sont approchés. Ont-ils faim, eux aussi ?

Parfois, on voit des animaux sauvages dans les jardins. Il y a de plus en plus de maisons, et avec cette nouvelle **URBANISATION**, ils sont un peu perdus.

Mais en fait... ils sont chez eux, ici,
et nous sommes les intrus !

« Clic ! »

Ils ne sont pas en VOIE DE DISPARITION et Pierre en croisera d'autres.

Mais leurs jolies silhouettes sont maintenant dans l'appareil photo, en souvenir de cette promenade et en attendant la prochaine.

Maman a promis de lui offrir un album pour son anniversaire. Il pourra y classer quelques images.

Les animaux rares ou lointains, il faudra les dessiner ! Pierre rêve souvent devant la télé : WOMBATS, XERUS... eux, il ne pourra jamais les observer.

Retour à la maison !
« Bonsoir, Monsieur Jo, et merci pour les haricots ! »

« De rien ! Et encore bravo au gang des Mains Vertes : vous allez au-delà des **Y A QU'À** que l'on entend si souvent. Allez, bonne soirée et bon repas ! »

Et le soir, dans son lit, Pierre s'évade loin de la petite ville, de la forêt si riche et du jardin de Monsieur Jo.

Il rêve de grands fauves, d'éléphants et de **ZEBRES**... mais pas dans un **Zoo**.

« Clic ! » À bientôt !

LE « GANG DES MAINS VERTES »

- Quelques gestes au quotidien -

Pierre et ses amis ont créé ce groupe au nom rigolo parce qu'ils pensent que chacun peut, chaque jour, améliorer la qualité de vie de tout le monde en faisant de petits gestes (qui ne coûtent rien !).
Comme eux, tu peux devenir un super-héros ou une super-héroïne de l'environnement.
Voici quelques idées très simples.

- En ville comme à la campagne, on ne jette pas ses déchets n'importe où (si tu en vois par terre, n'hésite pas à les ramasser pour les mettre dans la poubelle adaptée la plus proche).
Et on les trie !
Lorsque nous achetons de la nourriture ou d'autres choses en magasin, il y a presque toujours un emballage dont il faudra se débarrasser : apprends les règles de tri pour ne pas te tromper et être sûr(e) de le mettre dans la bonne poubelle. Il peut être recyclable, c'est à dire que la matière usée peut servir à produire autre chose ensuite (elle n'est pas « perdue »).

- Pour aller plus loin, pourquoi ne pas prendre un sac lorsque tu pars en promenade ?
Certaines personnes salissent, mais toi, tu peux faire une bonne action en nettoyant la nature...

Il y a, dans certaines régions, des opérations régulières de nettoyage des bords de rivières ou de fleuves. C'est notamment le cas en Normandie (pour les bords de Seine) mais il y a bien d'autres exemples. Les plages et les chemins de campagne sont aussi des endroits où tu peux faire la chasse aux emballages, bouteilles, papiers et autres choses sales.

- Parfois, ce que tu penses être un « déchet » peut être réutilisé.

Comme Flore, tu peux garder des choses en réserve parce qu'elles te seront peut-être utiles plus tard (emballages divers, cartons...) ou pour des petits bricolages. Il existe de très nombreux livres et des sites internet expliquant comment réaliser des objets en « récup' », pour la décoration, des jeux, des cadeaux personnalisés...

Et au jardin (ou sur ton balcon, ta terrasse...), ce que tu vas semer ou planter appréciera certainement l'engrais naturel que constitue le compost, à base de déchets alimentaires, du jardin etc. C'est aussi du recyclage !

- Pour rendre ton environnement plus agréable, tu peux aussi faire de petites plantations :

Des arbustes, des herbes aromatiques, des fleurs, c'est joli et utile ! On peut planter simplement chez soi ou dans des endroits où les fruits, les légumes et les herbes seront à la disposition de tout le monde. Une belle idée, qui progresse. Dans de plus en plus de villes et de villages, apparaissent des jardinières où pousse de la nourriture à partager. Cela permet à certaines personnes d'avoir des aliments sains et gratuits.

LA FORÊT ET LES MILIEUX FRAGILES

- Les connaître et les protéger -

La forêt est un milieu où vivent de nombreux animaux, au-dessus de la surface du sol (dans les herbes, les buissons, les arbres) ou sous cette surface ; on ne les voit donc pas tous, mais ils sont bien là et participent à ce que l'on appelle l' « équilibre naturel ».
Dans d'autres milieux, comme les rivières, les lacs, les océans... c'est pareil : les végétaux et les animaux forment un ensemble qui ne doit pas être perturbé.

- Les activités des hommes sont à l'origine de différentes pollutions, dans l'air ou dans l'eau. Parfois, nous détruisons l'habitat de certaines espèces ; elles deviennent alors plus rares et peuvent finir par disparaître.
Non seulement c'est triste, mais en plus, cela peut provoquer la disparition d'autres animaux, ou au contraire une forte augmentation de leur population. Il en est de même pour des plantes qui peuvent devenir envahissantes parce qu'elles « prennent la place » d'autres devenues rares.
Pour éviter ce déséquilibre, chacun doit faire un effort... qui parfois n'en est pas vraiment un puisqu'il suffit de veiller à la manière dont nous nous comportons.

- Nous ne parlerons pas ici d'autre chose que ces petits gestes que tu peux très facilement accomplir lorsque tu te promènes dans un environnement vivant. Et avant tout, renseigne-toi sur celui-ci !

Dans de nombreux lieux de visite ou de randonnée, il y a des points d'information. Avec l'aide des adultes, tu pourras apprendre plein de choses sur cet espace et donc, mieux le respecter.

Prenons par exemple le cas de la forêt, où se déroule une grande partie de l'action de ce livre.

- Reste le plus possible sur les chemins : les lieux de passage sont moins riches en végétation et en faune ; en restant bien dessus, tu ne détruiras rien et gêneras peu de petites bêtes !
- Ne fais pas trop de bruit et ne crie pas, pour ne pas effrayer inutilement les animaux.
- Jamais de feux en forêt ! Un barbecue ou un feu de camp, cela paraît sympathique mais c'est interdit : les risques d'incendie sont importants, surtout dans les régions sèches.
- Ne jette rien par terre ! La nature n'est pas une poubelle, garde tes déchets en poche ou dans ton sac jusqu'à ton retour chez toi.
- Cueille le moins possible, et n'arrache pas de branches ni de jeunes pousses : la végétation a besoin de se renouveler, ce qui n'est pas possible si tu abîmes ses parties « vivantes ». De plus, certaines espèces de plantes sont rares, il ne faut pas les cueillir.

D'une manière générale, essaie de ne pas déranger ce milieu et ses habitants...
Suivre ces quelques recommandations ne t'empêchera pas de profiter de tes promenades. Comme Pierre, tu peux photographier de jolis endroits ou des animaux que tu as eu la chance d'observer ; tu peux aussi prévoir des jumelles dans ton sac. N'hésite pas à coller ton oreille sur les troncs des arbres : ils te raconteront peut-être leurs secrets...

ESPECES EN DANGER !

- Des animaux à protéger -

Dans ce livre, plusieurs espèces animales ont été citées. Il y en a qui vivent dans des pays lointains (jaguar, koala, wombat, xérus, zèbre...) et d'autres que l'on observe plus près de chez nous. Ou du moins, que l'on essaie d'observer mais qui sont de moins en moins visibles !
Tu entends parfois parler d'espèces « menacées » ou « protégées » : qu'est-ce que c'est ?
Une espèce menacée risque de disparaître rapidement ou dans quelques dizaines d'années.
Une espèce protégée est un végétal ou un animal qui est considéré comme important, et donc bénéficie de lois spéciales concernant sa manipulation ou même son observation. Ce sont souvent des espèces déjà menacées dont on interdit la chasse, le transport, la vente, parfois l'approche ou la photographie.

On parle souvent de grands animaux ou de plantes, mais des insectes ou des champignons peuvent être concernés !
Dans ce cas, leur commerce est généralement interdit sous toutes ses formes (individus morts ou vivants, œufs, larves, viandes, produits dérivés...).

Tu ne l'imagines peut-être pas, mais il y a autour de toi de nombreuses espèces menacées et protégées.
- Chez les insectes, par exemple, plusieurs pollinisateurs (qui permettent aux plantes de se reproduire et aux fruits de se former) sont de plus en plus rares ; c'est notamment le cas des abeilles, tu en as certainement entendu parler. Mais il y a aussi la coccinelle européenne, pour d'autres raisons.

Pour elles, il y a des gestes simples que tu peux accomplir chez toi, même si cela ne remplace pas ce qui doit être fait à plus grande échelle (interdiction de certains produits chimiques pour les cultures, par exemple). Comme Flore, tu peux construire des abris à insectes, en plus de ne pas utiliser de pesticides pour tes plantations.

Pour un nid tout simple, il te faut :

- des tiges creuses sèches (dont un côté sera bouché en les trempant dans la boue, par exemple) de plusieurs diamètres
- des tiges pleines sèches (branches d'arbustes...)
- de la ficelle, du raphia ou du fil de fer

Tu constitues des petits fagots en attachant ces tiges, et tu les suspends dans ton jardin, sur ton balcon ou sur ta terrasse ; ces nichoirs seront des refuges pour de nombreuses espèces fragiles mais très utiles.

- Chez les petits mammifères, sais-tu que le hérisson est protégé en Europe depuis plusieurs dizaines d'années et que la loi a encore été renforcée il y a quelque temps ?
Ce petit animal sympathique est maintenant menacé de disparition, alors si tu en vois dans ton jardin, prends-en soin ! Des informations et des conseils sont donnés dans un autre livre : « Cours, petit hérisson ! ».

Tu y verras comment l'accueillir au mieux et l'aider. Pour lui aussi, tu peux préparer des gîtes (abris) afin qu'il passe sans problème la saison froide et que les familles survivent tout au long de l'année, car il est bien utile...

Cet ouvrage est imprimé en France par PRINTACHATS (Saint-Brieuc),
selon un procédé respectueux de l'environnement.

ISBN : 979-10-91893-19-0
Première édition
Achevé d'imprimer en août 2017
Dépôt légal : 3e trimestre 2017
Editeur : Vert Pomme
(75 La Mare Barbey - 76210 Saint-Eustache-la-Forêt)
Maquette : Séverine Dalla

Si la lecture de cet album vous inspire un commentaire,
n'hésitez pas : contact@vertpomme-editions.fr

Ce projet a bénéficié
du soutien de la Direction
Régionale des Affaires
Culturelles de Normandie

Conforme à la loi n° 49-956 du 16 juillet 1949 sur les publications destinées à la jeunesse,
modifiée par la loi n° 2011-525 du 17 mai 2011.

© Vert Pomme, 2017 - Reproduction interdite, pour tous supports et tous pays.

CW01657646

CONTENTS

PICTURE STRIPS AND STORIES

PUZZLES AND GAMES

FEATURES

Written and produced by Angus P. Allan.
Copyright © MCMLXXVII by Associated Television Limited.
All rights reserved throughout the world.
Published in Great Britain by World Distributors
(Manchester) Limited. A Member of the Pentos Group.
P.O. Box 111, 12 Lever Street, Manchester M60 1TS.
Printed in Great Britain by Jarrold and Sons Ltd., Norwich.
SBN 7235 0431 8

message from John Koenig, commanding Moonbase Alpha. distribution: ALL READERS.

Welcome once again to Moonbase Alpha! There've been several changes since we last met up - and we've been through one heck of a lot! In the following pages, you'll read about some of it - and meet new people. We want to start off by giving you the lowdown on what was possibly our most dramatic adventure . . . but why should I say more? Just turn over and read on!

ENTER THE METAMORPH!

"Moonbase Alpha. Status report. One hundred and eight days since leaving orbit. Doctor Helena Russell recording. We have just survived our second encounter with a space warp. Central computer states that we have catapulted six light years from our last position. Survey Eagles are reconnoitering a planet in an attempt to locate Tiranium – a rare metal used in the repair of our life-support systems..."

Those were the bald facts, as put on tape by Alpha Chief Medical Officer, just one of the people marooned in space after the massive nuclear explosion that had torn the Moon free of Earth's protective hold.

Bald facts that began the unfolding of a dramatic story. A terrifying adventure that was to bring them a new ally at the very moment they were threatened with total extinction! An ally with powers beyond their wildest dreams...

Commander John Koenig stood rigid with tension in Main Mission, his eyes glued to the big video screen in front of him. On it, the clear image of Survey Eagle One, skimming above the rocky surface of the alien planet. Pilots Fraser and Torens had that moment reported breathable atmosphere. More important, the presence of the vital mineral Tiranium, so necessary to the Alphans' survival!

But now, in the very moment that he'd given them the order to return to base, Koenig saw a ball of green fire materialise from a mountain outcrop. Saw it swell and grow, rising from the ground to pursue the Eagle!

"There's a strange light on your tail! *Get out of there!"*

Fraser grabbed the controls and hurled them forward, feeling the thrust as the engines of his craft surged to full power. In a wild series of twisting turns, the Eagle tried desperately to shake off its attacker . . . but to no avail! It caught up. Engulfed. And the last thing Koenig heard was Fraser's feeble call for help as, motors cancelled, the Eagle was drawn helplessly back to the planet's surface.

Within seconds, Koenig had ordered maximum alert. Combat Eagles rose from their launch pads. Defensive force shields were in position and ready. The huge laser batteries were armed and uncovered. Moonbase Alpha was ready to fight!

It was at that moment that the big video screen dimmed for a split instant, then returned to life

. . . this time with the facial image of a proud, intelligent, bearded face upon it. There was absolute silence in Main Mission as the full, humorous lips opened to speak.

"Commander Koenig!"

Koenig sat down heavily. "You – you know who I am . . .?"

"I am Mentor, of the planet Psychon."

Back on balance now, the Moonbase Commander kept his voice level.

"Why did you attack our ship? It was merely a survey vessel, looking for minerals. We thought your world was uninhabited."

Mentor sighed. "A familiar statement, Commander. One which has caused the death of millions of our people. Other outsiders have used the same pretext to attack us in the past."

"What happened to *my* people?" ground out Koenig.

"Your pilots are safe. But their Eagle is beyond repair."

"Return my men, Mentor. And we will go in peace. That's what you want, obviously. You have my solemn pledge that no hostile action will be taken."

Mentor nodded slowly. "I accept your pledge. Send another Eagle, and I shall instruct it where to land."

Koenig glanced about him. The eyes of his colleagues – Sandra Benes – Tony Verdeschi – David Kano – all of them said a silent 'no'.

"It seems you trust us as little as we trust you, Commander," smiled Mentor. "We shall meet in space."

Transmission closed down, and Koenig gave orders for Eagle Four to be fitted with additional booster units and placed on its pad. He chose Helena Russell, Alan Carter and Lew Picard to accompany him, and hoped fervently that he wasn't condemning them to death. For all he knew, this Mentor was capable of treachery!

And on the planet Psychon, the bearded man, still smiling thinly to himself, turned from his video-transmitter and spoke softly to the sleek, feline shape of a lion that curled on a divan.

"Well, Maya. What do you think of these Alphans. . ?"

A glow came to the animal's eyes. Reflected in the pupils for an instant was the languid figure of a beautiful girl. And then, abruptly, the lion vanished, and the girl herself uncoiled from the divan! For this – Mentor's daughter – had the power to assume any shape at will. She was – the Metamorph!

Rocks on the alien planet had begun to glow with green light. In the flicker of an eye, a huge spaceship materialised at the centre of the radiation, and now the vessel began its climb through the Psychonian atmosphere.

In Eagle Four, Koenig and his colleagues were waiting. Nervously they watched its approach.

"Mentor!" Koenig spoke rapidly into the transceiver. "Signal when you're ready to dock!"

But there was no reply, and the Commander felt the hairs on his neck rise as the urgent face of his Moonbase Controller flashed up on the monitor.

"John! There are no life-forms on that ship! Fraser – Torens – they're not aboard! The thing's completely *empty!*"

It was too late for Koenig to take evasive action. Some kind of magnetic force radiated from the alien craft. It drew the Eagle inexorably towards it. Held it fast like a giant magnet. And then began to drop back towards Psychon, the four Alphans helpless prisoners!

Koenig, Helena, Alan and Lew sat rigid in total silence as they were lowered to the planet's surface. In through the jagged circle of a crater, perhaps of a long-extinct volcano. Then, below them, through swirling mists, they saw them – the rusting shapes of a hundred spaceships. A bewildering variety of craft lying in twisted desolation!

"A graveyard! A cemetery of the spaceways," breathed Alan Carter. "And we're being dumped right in the middle of it!"

Nothing hindered Koenig and his friends as they warily left their Eagle. No force struck them down. It was Helena who first discovered the cavern entrance that led downwards from the crater's surface, and it was Alan Carter, stun-gun drawn, who led the way.

Through twisting rock passages, their path took them in a seemingly endless spiral – until, abruptly, they emerged in a vast cavern, where beings toiled with pick and basket, chipping remorselessly away at the rocks around them.

"The crews of the crashed ships, Commander?" Lew Picard's question was more of a statement.

Koeing nodded grimly. "And look at them. Zombies, all of them. They don't even sense our presence!"

Carter's hand fell suddenly on Koenig's arm, the fingers painful with tension. "Look, John! *Look!*"

It was pilot Torens. Co-flyer of Survey Eagle One. And he was just like the rest. A glassy-eyed automaton, streaked with dirt, a mindless slave toiling in Mentor's mine!

Koenig jumped towards him, hands outstretched. And a blast of energy as quickly hurled him back at the feet of his companions!

"Nnuhhh! Some – sort of force-field around him. . ." Koenig clambered dizzily to his feet. "We've got to get out of here – before we suffer the same fate!"

"We can't *leave* Torens!" Helena's voice was shrill with horror.

"No." Koenig shook his head, slowly. "First, we locate Mentor!"

And then, from behind them, came the hurried footfalls that made them spin round, guns at the ready! The weird, helmeted humanoids with rifles of their own – rifles that spat streams of energy in blasting, destructive force!

Alan and Helena had no chance. Koenig saw them fall even as his own weapon spat death at the attackers! His shot struck home, and for an instant, a green glow enveloped his target. Then it vanished as though it had never been there!

The Commander just had time to hear Picard, his voice at panic-level, scream, "Molecular transformation! Creatures conjured out of nothing!" And then came oblivion as something slammed him in the chest and stretched him senseless on the ground!

Koenig awoke to find himself lying amidst a mind-boggling array of electronic consoles, each surmounted with a cluster of thick transparent cylinders, in which multi-coloured liquids boiled and bubbled. His mind struggled to try and grasp their meaning. And then came Mentor's voice. . .

"It's called Psyche, Commander. A biological computer."

The bearded man was smiling down at him, and Koenig eased himself to his feet. He was aware of another presence. Turned to look into the deep, almost violet eyes of Maya.

"Welcome, Commander John Koenig," she said. "I am Maya. Mentor's daughter. Oh – please don't worry about your friends. They're quite safe."

"If you're as trustworthy as

your father," snarled Koenig, "you'll forgive me for not believing you!"

Maya looked distressed. For a moment, she glanced nervously at Mentor, but he smiled reassuringly.

"Please, Koenig," he said, "you misjudge us. Look." He struck a switch on a nearby panel, and a glass wall behind him became transparent. Beyond it, Koenig saw Helena and Alan, in chairs, with one of the strange, helmeted guards behind them. They looked anxious, but unharmed.

"They cannot see *us,* "explained Mentor. "And the others are in a similar chamber." He turned off the switch.

"What about Torens?" said Koenig. "I saw him down there with those others. Those aliens you've enslaved!"

Maya frowned. "What's he talking about, father?"

Mentor made a throwaway gesture. "He's suffered some kind of delusion, my dear. Pay no attention. In fact, perhaps you'd leave us now. The Commander and I have much to discuss."

When the girl had gone, Mentor turned to the mass of bubbling pipes he'd called Psyche, his biological computer. His voice took on the intense, quavering note of the true fanatic.

"See, Koenig! All this – created from the minds and bodies of those of our people who survived the disaster which overwhelmed us! They live on, just waiting for the time when I can re-create them in bodily form!"

Koenig felt numb. "Those zombies in your mines. You've taken their minds. Their intelligence. To feed into this – this *thing!* In an attempt to revive your own race!"

"Exactly, Commander! Psyche *feeds* on intelligence." He paused. "And that is why I need the minds of your Alphans. All of them! With such a supply of intellect, my dream can come true!"

"You – you must be crazy!" John Koenig could only gape at the man. "You think *I'll* agree to your monstrous suggestion?"

"You'll have no choice. You see, your refusal will mean that I shall totally destroy your Moon. And believe me – I have the power to do it!"

Koenig sagged. He knew now that Helena and the others were far from safe. That they were due, all of them, to have their minds sucked dry. To be fed into Psyche. That they'd end up like human robots, to dig out the metal needed for the biological computer's physical structure. And yet there was one shred of hope in the Commander's mind. The realisation that Mentor's daughter Maya didn't know. Didn't realise exactly what her father was up to. Otherwise, why should she have been uncertain? Why had she been banished while Mentor told Koenig the ghastly truth. . ?

"If we're going to escape from here," thought Koenig, "it's *got* to be with Maya's aid!"

The chance came sooner than Koenig expected. To gain Mentor's confidence, he had pretended to agree to the man's demands. In return for the guarantee of his own life. Helena and the others, who indeed knew the fate that awaited them, could hardly believe it as they heard Koenig get into direct touch with Moonbase Alpha and give controller Tony Verdeschi the order to evacuate all personnel down to Psychon.

"It's safe, and we have permission to colonise, Tony," he'd said. "Instigate Operation Exodus immediately. Directive Four."

On Alpha, Tony and the others made *no* plans to quit the Moon. For Tony knew that Directive Four was a code signal. A signal that meant 'destroy source of origin'. Heavy hearted, he made ready the robot Eagle that would send a chain-reaction bomb down to Psychon. To destroy it utterly. Along with his Commander. Along with Helena and the rest. There could be no questioning that directive. Koenig himself had given it, knowing that there was no other way to avert the danger that threatened Moonbase and its personnel.

And Koenig's chance? He knew well that Mentor would spot the robot bomb almost as soon as it was launched. Would explode with fury at the attempted treachery!

It happened. His face a mask of anger, Mentor contemptuously released the ray that blasted the Eagle to bits in mid flight.

"Now, Commander! Now – your Moon! You shall watch it disintegrate!"

"No," said Koenig. "Let's negotiate."

It was Maya who spoke, her voice thick with revulsion. "Negotiate? With a *liar?* We welcome you here as friends, and you plot to kill us!"

Evenly, Koenig said: "What are we supposed to do? Stand by and let Mentor destroy *us?"*

"My father needs your *help,"* the girl snapped. "Without it, he can't transform this planet! *Others* helped him!"

"Yes – and what *happened* to them? Go down to the mines! See for yourself!"

"I can't go down there! It's a radioactive zone!"

Koenig smiled viciously. "Who told you that? Your *father?"*

Mentor stood with his mouth agape. He seemed incapable of movement. Maya, her eyes full of tears, spun on her heel and ran from the room, and Koenig threw himself at the bearded man to stop him following. To stop him bringing her back!

Mentor possessed immense strength. Koenig felt his senses swimming as they rolled together on the floor, bony fingers locked into his throat! And then the shattering crash of glass as their flailing legs came into contact with one of the multi-cylinder structures of Psyche! Blue liquid sprayed out – drenched them. . .

With a strangled cry, Mentor released his grip on the Commander and staggered to his feet, his eyes starting from their sockets. "You fool! You *fool!"*

Now the Psychonian was babbling, his hands cut and bleeding as he tried in vain to restack the smashed equipment.

"Release Psyche's energy and it will *destroy* the planet!"

Koenig had picked up a chair. Now he threw it through the glass screen that separated him from Helena and the others. They raced out to join him, their guard immobile as Psyche's confusion left him without means of control.

And then Maya returned, her face ashen. "This way! Come on!"

Mentor cowered back. "Maya! What are you *doing!* Kill them! Annihilate them!"

"I saw, father! I *saw!"* There was anguish in the girl's voice. The memories of that dreadful mine were still stamped on her mind! "Come with us, father! It's *over!"*

Psyche bubbled and boiled. Now flashes of energy began to race from terminal to terminal. Minor explosions rocked the whole structure and shattered fresh columns . . . unleashed more and more power! Mentor collapsed, buried under a deluge of crushing masonry that fell from above him!

They were running. Down through the mine. Over the shaking, pounding rock. Past the witless zombies who continued to chip and hew as though nothing was happening. . .

"Torens! Fraser!" Helena was screaming. "Where *are* they?"

"Beyond our help, Helena! *We* could never return them their minds!" Koenig grabbed her wrist and dragged her headlong. . .

The Eagle lifted away from the volcano's crater, its engines at full thrust. It left behind it a planet in its death-throes. A planet doomed to utter destruction, because of the ruthless ambition of one man. . .

And with it, it carried the sole survivor of the Psychonian race. A girl called Maya. A girl whose shattered faith in her own father might have taken her beyond the brink of sanity. And yet she would recover. Would adjust and adapt. To become a new and valued colleague of Commander John Koenig and the castaway people of Moonbase Alpha. . .

Chief pilot, Moonbase Alpha -

ALAN CARTER

LSRO

Maya– miracle girl!

Because she knows the secrets of molecular transformation, Maya has the uncanny ability to change her shape at will. To become, instantly, another human being. To turn herself into an animal of any kind. Even into a tree, a rock, or a monster. An astounding accomplishment for this beautiful alien who has become a science officer on Moonbase Alpha, her computer-like brain a valuable added weapon in the fight for survival of John Koenig and his people.

The search for the most fabulous female of all time necessitated testing 154 actresses of numerous nationalities for the part – and Catherine Schell was chosen.

This tall Hungarian-born actress won high praise for her performance in the Peter Sellers comedy 'Return Of The Pink Panther' – one of the many films and television shows in which she has attracted attention.

By coincidence, her first major role in a British film was in 'Moon Two Zero', in which she portrayed a girl who went to the Moon in search of her missing astronaut brother.

Catherine is the daughter of the Baron and Baroness Schell Von Bauschlott, but her father renounced his title when the family fled to The United States during Hungary's post-war political upheaval. She was educated in Washington and New York, then in Munich, Germany. "So," she says, "I can't help feeling that I'm aptly cast as Maya because I, too, am an alien. A foreigner in every country. I have an American passport and a British resident permit, but wherever I go, I can't feel that I really belong."

Catherine enrolled as a drama student after school, took part in a radio play, and made a brief appearance in a film before going to Brazil to play her first lead in 'Lana, Queen Of The Amazons'. After this, she was based in Munich with her family, but filmed all over Europe and elsewhere.

Of her role as Maya, Catherine says: "I have feline looks, and my make-up is marvellous. Transforming myself into all sorts of other creatures is intriguing, and to help in these changes I have to study the animals and other creatures beforehand so that I can slip into poses which suggest them, and make the transformations appear more real. I've been learning to crouch, snarl and growl! *That's* something they never taught me at drama school!"

A tense moment in Main Mission for Maya – pictured here with controller Tony Verdeschi, played by Tony Anholt.

A MEANS FOR REVENGE!

The small, coffin-shaped metal cannister had appeared suddenly. A mere speck in space that might have passed un-noticed save for the ultra-sophisticated probe equipment in Main Mission. Together, Commander John Koenig and Chief Pilot Alan Carter had taken Eagle Two to investigate, and now, even as they drew near, their ears were blasted by a sudden, shrieking transmission that seemed to fill every inch of their craft!

That it came from the strange object there could be no doubt. And it was just as certain that they were powerless against it! Such was the intensity of that fearful noise that it shook at the foundations of their very minds. Blocked their reflex impulses. Paralysed their nervous systems so that they could only sit contorted with agony, their hands clamped in vain over their jangling ears! Within seconds, both of them passed mercifully into total unconsciousness!

In Main Mission, Controller Tony Verdeschi rose from his desk and strode across to the big video screen. Neither he nor his colleagues had heard anything of the shattering din that had overcome pilot and commander, but audio contact with the Eagle had naturally been lost.

"Commander! Come in! Do you copy? Can you hear me?"

David Kano turned from the computer. "Must be some technical fault. The Eagle's okay . . . look."

Sure enough, the big screen clearly showed Eagle Two turning from its objective, to begin its run for home.

"Standby Medical unit to docking area," snapped Verdeschi. "Just in case."

Doctor Helena Russell and her team were ready at the interior airlock even as the Eagle landed. And long minutes ticked by.

"What's keeping them?" This from her assistant, Doctor Mathias. "Do you reckon we ought to suit up and go out there . . ?"

But then the airlock doors slid open, and the medical team were startled into frozen amazement. Yes, Koenig and Carter were there – but limp in the grasp of a tall, swarthy alien, his powerful chest banded with golden straps.

"Who – who the blazes . . ?" Mathias was the first to recover his speech.

The alien smiled, not without a trace of nervousness as he looked about him. "I am Vamar," he said, simply. "I very much regret what has happened to your friends!"

"Are they . . ?" Helena's face was an ashen mask.

"Oh, no. Not dead," said Vamar hastily. "Believe me, they will recover. I fear they were stunned by the protective radiation from my capsule."

"*You* flew the Eagle back here . . ?"

Vamar nodded. "Luckily, the controls were within my sphere of understanding. Er – should you not take these men to your hospital . . ?"

It was a full twenty minutes before Commander Koenig and Alan had recovered sufficiently for them to greet the alien who had brought them home. Helena Russell accompanied them to the anteroom where Maya had already been interviewing him.

"His story's quite a shocker, John," said Maya. "He says he was the ruler of a planet called Tal, until he was deposed in a revolution . . ."

"A ruthless and warlike faction took over," said Vamar. "I was sent for trial, and condemned to be sealed in that capsule and cast out into space, to drift for ever in a kind of suspended animation. It was sheer good fortune for me that you found me, Commander – and you have my thanks. My eternal thanks."

Koenig shook his head. "And you have mine, Vamar. If you hadn't taken control of our Eagle, that sonic force might well have damaged our minds beyond hope of repair."

Vamar smiled modestly. "You are wondering, perhaps, how I came aboard? Again, it was pure chance that brought my capsule against your airlock entrance and opened it. Otherwise . . ." He shrugged, expressively.

"Yes. That was *very* lucky," murmured Maya under her breath. And a slow frown gathered for a moment on her forehead . . .

Koenig had given the order for suitable quarters to be made available for their new guest. The alien's friendliness had already made him popular with the command personnel. Only Maya, with her superbly tuned senses, harboured a niggling doubt about him. Something she could neither place nor justify. Was he perhaps *too* amiable? *Too* quiet and self-effacing? But she kept her doubts to herself.

Vamar had entered Main Mission. Had asked to see the star-chart of the Moon's present position.

"Yes. I see." He glanced quizzically at Koenig. "Your course will take you within reach of my planet, Commander," he said. "There *are* people loyal to me on Tal. Would there be the remotest possibility . . ?"

"You want me to get you back there, Vamar? We have the resources here for the construction of replacement Eagles. I see no reason why I shouldn't provide you with one. However, I must make it clear that I cannot, under any circumstance whatever, involve my people in any kind of alien power-struggle. If you return to Tal, you must do so alone."

Vamar looked shocked. "My dear Commander! I would not dream of asking you to give me any sort of military assistance. That would be absolutely unthinkable!"

Koenig was satisfied. Not so Maya. She had seen a flicker – of amusement, perhaps? A glint deep in Vamar's eyes that gave the hint of treachery. She turned and left Main Mission ahead of him, and went straight to his quarters.

There, alone and unseen, Maya turned her mind to the astonishing means of transfiguration of which she was capable. She concentrated on a spider – and in the blink of an eye, became one. Tiny and insignificant. The perfect means of eavesdropping – of watching Vamar's every movement without the slightest risk of discovery!

She saw the alien return. Noted with satisfaction that the ingratiating smile was gone from his face. That it had been replaced with a look of vicious ugliness! Better still – the man was in the habit of talking to himself!

Muttered undertones. So that Maya had to strain her hearing to listen. But she heard clearly enough!

"The fools," said Vamar. "They have believed every word I told them! Yes, I shall return to Tal, and deal such a blow that they will tremble at the name of Vamar for ever . . . *if* any of them survive to do so! How obliging of Koenig to put an Eagle at my disposal! Little does the idiot realise that it will be armed! Armed with one of the chain reaction nuclear bombs that I saw when he was stupid enough to allow me free roam through his Alphan complex!"

Vamar strode from his quarters, and instantly, Maya resumed her own form. At a discreet distance, she followed the alien as he made straight for the life-support centre that was the hub of Moonbase Alpha! "When the time comes," muttered Vamar, "some sabotage here will give them all far too much to worry about to bother with me!"

"That's just where you're wrong, Vamar!" Maya's whiplash voice brought the alien spinning round, his jaw dropping with amazement! Then he was on her – his supple body possessed of fantastic strength!

Maya fought like a tigress. Given one more second, and she could have become one! But Vamar's hands were locked around her throat, and her senses reeled blackly! A gasping scream tried to force its way between her drawn lips . . .

Then Vamar was torn bodily from her, and as she sank dizzily to the floor, she heard the solid crack of fist against bone. John Koenig's fist!

Vamar reeled away from the Commander, to fetch up against an equipment console with stunning force. Yet the alien hurled himself back to the attack, murder in his eyes!

"You'll be sorry for this, Koenig! You and all your people!"

Winded by the man's rush, Koenig gave ground, every ounce of his strength pitted against Vamar's incredible muscular power.

It was only the Commander's old judo training that saved him. For a split second, he slumped, taking his adversary off balance. Then he pivoted on his heels and used the man's own momentum to swing him clear into the air and hurl him across the room!

A throw that would have probably broken a normal human being's neck. Would at least have finished the fight. But Vamar was almost impossibly

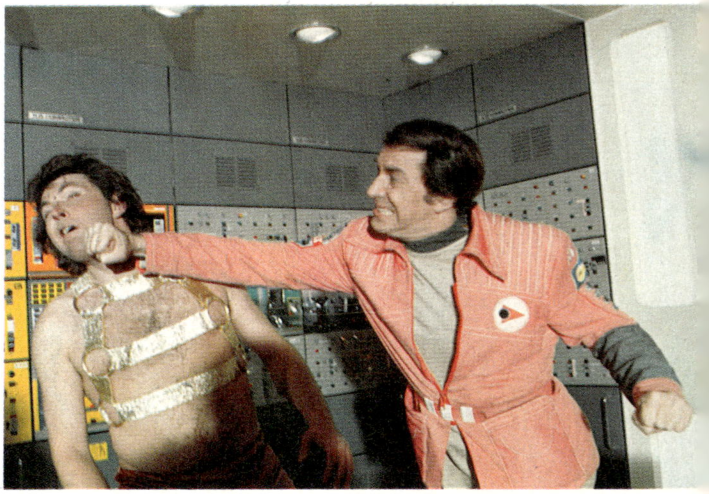

agile! Body balled like an acrobat's, he landed on his feet, and next second he'd sprinted through the open doorway!

"All units!" Breathlessly, Koenig triggered the comlock that put him in immediate touch with every section of Alpha. "Vamar is an enemy. Repeat – an enemy! Stun on sight and detain!"

Then the Commander stooped to lift the dazed girl to her feet.

"John! How – how did you . . ?"

"He tripped a security beam when he came in here, Maya. I saw him on video – with you about to try and jump him. Now quickly – what happened?"

Maya explained what she'd overheard, and Koenig whistled softly. "My stars! If he'd got away with it! He'd have unleashed chaos on Tal . . . and they'd probably have sent all kinds of hate up at us in retaliation! The mind boggles!"

Together, they ran to Main Mission. Where Sandra

Benes had even more to report!

"We've pinpointed Tal, Commander. Deep video probe shows it to be inhabited, but spectroscan says the people aren't humanoid. They're not Vamar's race at all!"

Koenig gritted his teeth. "I can guess the story. Vamar's probably some kind of enemy of theirs. Maybe the leader of some attempted invasion. He was banished to space alright – but because he was a warmongering belligerent. And he hoped to use us as an instrument of revenge!"

Suddenly, Koenig was aware of Tony Verdeschi's hand on his arm, the fingers tightly and tensely locked. He swivelled to look into the man's horrified face.

"John! He's got to the missile Eagles! He's got there, and the security squad can't touch him! *He's taken Helena as a hostage*!"

Her mind racing, Helena Russell sat in the co-pilot's seat of Eagle Seven, where Vamar had thrown her. The alien was beside her, gloating with triumph, for Eagle Seven was the emergency craft kept bombed-up at all times with one of the most sophisticated of Alphan weapons – the chain-reaction bomb that had the power of destruction on a mammoth scale!

"Your friends will not sacrifice *you*, doctor," snarled Vamar. "Oh dear no. They will doubtless try bargaining. Persuading. As if *I* will heed their ridiculous pleading!"

"You're mad, Vamar. Quite mad. Even with such a missile, you can't hope to subdue a whole planet alone!"

"But I can, lady! I *can!* Now – tell them yourself. Tell them to put this Eagle on its launch pad . . . or you suffer!"

Sheer despair drove Helena to one violent, desperate attempt to swing the balance! Heedlessly, she threw herself at Vamar, fingers clawing for his face!

And then it happened! As they grappled, Vamar's own arm came down on the impulse levers of the

"You fool!" Helena's voice rose to a wild shriek. "We're on fire!"

Eagle's firing mechanisms, and ignition pinwheels within the powerful motors burst into life!

The result was immediate. Within the docking bay, all engine vents were sealed. So that the instant overload blew the electrical circuits, and the whole control panel of the craft burst into lurid flame!

"You – you *fool*!" Helena's voice rose to a wild shriek! "We're on *fire*!"

Vamar lost his head. With a strangled yell, he tore loose from Helena, and she lost him in the acrid smoke that was rapidly filling the cabin. Choking and gasping, she fought her own way back to the exit and stumbled out into the arms of the ashen security men.

"Get – get clear! For pity's sake, *get clear*!"

Airlock doors slid closed behind them, and then they were racing for the travel tube. In minutes, Helena was back in Main Mission. "The bomb, John! The *bomb*!"

There wasn't a second to lose! Remotely, the stricken Eagle was raised to launch position. Equally remotely, the emergency thrusters were brought into play, and the craft lifted away from its pad – the eyes of everyone in Alpha's command-centre riveted to its image on the big video screen.

"Raise all protective shields," snapped Koenig. "Full radiation screen! Stand by for red-scale concussion!"

Gradually, the Eagle receded – a self-contained furnace that had already consumed its treacherous occupant, and now threatened the stability of the massive central missile!

The blast as it exploded shook the Moon to its very core. It was if a giant fist had gripped Alpha and shaken it – and the occupants of Main Mission were flung headlong like dolls! But with nothing in empty space to feed on, the chain reaction stopped as soon as it had begun, and there was only blackness, and a drift of dust. All that remained of Eagle Seven.

"I wonder if they picked that up on Tal," said Maya soberly.

"Probably," said Koenig. "But they'll never be able to figure out what caused it. How could they guess that it was Vamar's intended means of revenge . . ."

SPOT THE DIFFERENCE

The pictures below are identical – or are they? In fact, the bottom picture has ten small changes. So see if you can spot them! Answers, page 61.

THIS GREEN, UNPLEASANT LAND...

MOMENTS LATER...
AT MAXIMUM SPEED, THE EAGLE HURTLES DOWN INTO EARTH'S ATMOSPHERE...
LOOK THERE, ALAN! EUROPE!
OUR COURSE IS GOING TO TAKE US LOW OVER THE BRITISH ISLES, JOHN. BUT NO RADIO RESPONSE..? MAYBE THE WHOLE PLANET'S DEAD!
THEIR FIRST CLEAR VIEW SEEMS TO JUSTIFY THAT THEORY. THEY SEE THE THAMES... AND SOMETHING THAT ONCE WAS LONDON.
DESOLATION! UTTER DESOLATION!
SHALL I PUT HER DOWN, COMMANDER? THERE'S CLEAR GROUND ON THE HILLS NORTH OF THE RIVER...
I DID TWO YEARS OF STUDY IN ENGLAND, ALAN. THIS USED TO BE HAMPSTEAD HEATH...
I KNOW IT. I WAS HERE FOR A SPELL ON VACATION FROM AUSSIE...

WELCOME TO EARTH, MAYA. THE GARDEN'S GOT A BIT OUT OF HAND SINCE WE LEFT IT...
NO MOVEMENT! NOTHING!
SLITHER!
KREEEPPP!
IT'S—IT'S SO QUIET, ALAN. AND, I DON'T KNOW—I SENSE SOMETHING—MALIGNANT!
BETTER TAKE OFF AGAIN FOR A WIDER LOOK.
KLAMMP!
NYEEAAAGH!
ALAN! LOOK OUT!
GOOD GRIEF!
THRAMMMM!
SKRARRSSSH!
KOENIG'S GUN HAS LITTLE BUT LOCAL EFFECT! IT'S MAYA, WITH HER INCREDIBLE POWER OF METABOLISTIC TRANSFER, WHO SEES THE ONLY HOPE!

SNARRRRR!
RIPPPP!
SPRUNNNC
MERELY BY WILLING IT SO, SHE BECOMES A GORILLA!
SECONDS LATER, ALAN IS FREE, AND MAYA RETURNS TO HER NORMAL SELF...
MY STARS! THAT THING HAD A GRIP LIKE A VICE.
THRASSSSSA!
WE'D BETTER GET THE BLAZES OUT OF HERE! I'LL TAKE THE CONTROLS.
THE EAGLE HEADS NORTH. PAST THE RUINS OF CITIES LIKE BIRMINGHAM. DERBY. MANCHESTER. ALL OVERGROWN IN THE SAME WAY AS LONDON. CARLISLE. EDINBURGH. AND THEN OPEN COUNTRY...
NO GIANT SUNDEWS HERE, COMMANDER! OKAY TO PUT HER DOWN?
DO THAT.
IT LOOKS PEACEFUL-BUT BE READY FOR ANYTHING! THERE USED TO BE WHAT THEY CALLED 'BONNY PURPLE HEATHER' HERE... BUT NOT ANY MORE!

VICIOUS BARBS SLICE THE THICK MATERIAL! AND EVEN AS KOENIG FEELS ONE SCRATCH HIS FLESH...
YE GODS!
JOHN! THE VEGETATION'S MOVING! IT'S USING IT'S THORNS TO SLASH AT YOUR BOOTS!
NNNFFF!
HE'S COLLAPSED! GET HIM BACK INSIDE! CLOSE THE DOORS.
HE'S NOT BREATHING! QUICK, MAYA! EMERGENCY RESUSCITATOR!
HEART STIMULANT INJECTION, ALAN! HURRY!
MY OATH! THE WHOLE PLANET'S CRAZY! EARTH'S BECOME A PLAYGROUND FOR KILLER PLANTS!
MEANWHILE IN THE DIM DEPTHS OF A CAVERN NOT HALF A MILE AWAY...
THERE ARE PEOPLE OUTSIDE! PEOPLE LIKE US! THEY CAME IN A STRANGE CRAFT LIKE SOMETHING FROM THE OLD BOOKS!
THE-THE RETURNING ONES? MARGAN SAID LAST NIGHT THAT THERE WAS A MAN IN THE SKY!
JUST LIKE THE ONE OUR ANCESTORS WROTE ABOUT!

WHAT DO WE DO? THE PLANTS ARE OVERWHELMING THEM!
WE DO NOTHING! THERE IS NO ROOM FOR THEM HERE NOR ANYWHERE! THE EARTH THEY KNEW HAS GONE FOREVER... THANKS TO THEIR OWN FOOLISHNESS!
WHAT DO YOU MEAN GRANDFATHER?
WE WERE ONCE A RACE OF TECHNICIANS, MY BOY. SCIENTISTS AND INVENTORS WHO BROUGHT ABOUT THE DESTRUCTION OF THE WHOLE HUMAN RACE. WE ARE HUNDREDS, WHERE ONCE THERE WERE MILLIONS...
WE ARE THE LAST SURVIVORS... AND WE TOO ARE DYING OUT, FOR NATURE HAS DECREED THAT THE VEGETABLE KINGDOM NOW HAS ITS CHANCE TO INHERIT THE WORLD...
"THE ANIMALS WE CATCH TO SUSTAIN US-EVEN THEY FALL VICTIM TO THE PLANTS WHICH COVER OUR FORMER LANDS..."
COME AWAY, JORUS. DON'T PESTER YOUR GRANDFATHER. THESE OUTSIDERS ARE NO CONCERN OF OURS. THEY HAVE NO PART IN OUR FADING RACE...
AND IN THE EAGLE, WHERE COMMANDER KOENIG HAS BEEN REVIVED FROM THE EFFECTS OF THE POISONOUS THORNS...
NO USE... ALAN, THIS EARTH ISN'T FOR US! I CAN'T IMAGINE WHAT'S HAPPENED TO IT...
YEAH, COMMANDER. BUT IT DOESN'T WANT TO LET US GO! WE'RE TRAPPED TIGHT, AND THE THRUSTER PORTS ARE ALL BLOCKED!

IF I TRIGGER MAXIMUM THRUST, WE COULD BLOW OURSELVES TO SMITHEREENS!
WE'RE GOING TO BE UNCOMFORTABLY HOT FOR A MOMENT OR TWO. IT WON'T BE PLEASANT, BUT IT'S OUR ONLY CHANCE...
OKAY. I UNDERSTAND. ENGINES ARE READY TO GO.
KOENIG TO MOONBASE ALPHA! CANCEL PROJECT EXODUS. EARTH ENVIRONMENT HOSTILE.
REPEAT, HOSTILE. LAUNCH RELIEF EAGLE TWO TO ZERO ON THIS POINT, ARMED WITH FLAME UNIT...
EAGLE ONE CAN ONLY DIRECT THE RELIEF SHIP BY RADIO SIGNALS AS IT BORES IN FOR THE ATTACK...
STAND BY, COMMANDER! FIRING—NOW!
VA-ROOOMMMFFFF!

CLEAR FOR LIFT-OFF!
ESCAPED! THEY AND ANOTHER! OUR OLD MEN SAID TO IGNORE THEM. COULD WE HAVE MADE CONTACT..? GOT THEM TO TAKE US WITH THEM..?
IT WAS NOT TO BE. THEIR LIVES AND OURS MUST BE FOREVER SEPARATE AS DECREED BY FATE...
EAGLE ONE TO ALPHA. WE'RE COMING IN. TELL ALL UNITS. HOME ISN'T HOME ANY MORE. IT MAY BE GREEN, BUT IT'S A MOST UNPLEASANT LAND...

MOON-BEAMS

SOME OF THESE GUYS'LL DO **ANYTHING** FOR KICKS...

TAKE US TO YOUR LEADER!

I'VE TOLD YOU BEFORE ABOUT PLAYING WITH MATCHES, JOHNNY!

THIS ONE SAYS ARSENAL 6 SPURS 0

I **LIKE** YOU, HELENA! YOU'RE – **DIFFERENT**...

AND THIS IS OUR ECONOMY MODEL, SIR...

SPOT THE DIFFERENCE

The pictures below are identical – or are they? In fact, the bottom picture has ten small changes. So see if you can spot them! Answers, page 61.

TALKDOWN

A GAME FOR TWO OR MORE PLAYERS!

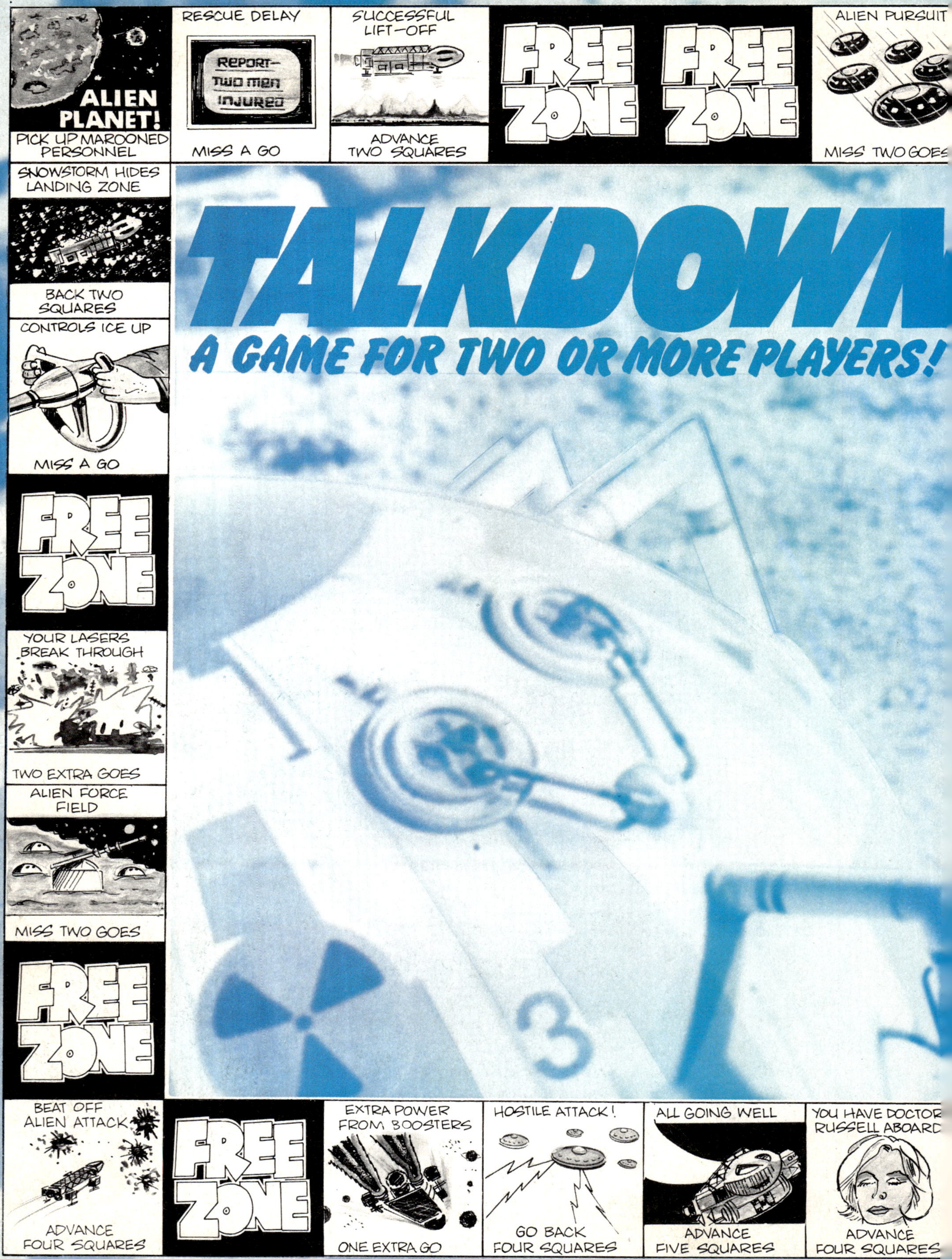

THE OBJECT OF THE GAME IS TO BE THE FIRST PLAYER TO FLY A RESCUE EAGLE TO AN ICEBOUND ALIEN PLANET, PICK UP A PARTY OF ALPHANS MAROONED THERE, AND THEN RETURN SAFELY TO MOONBASE! YOU'LL NEED A DICE, AND A COUNTER FOR EACH PLAYER. BUTTONS WILL DO AS LONG AS YOU REMEMBER WHICH IS YOURS! BEGIN FROM THE START SQUARE AND MOVE YOUR COUNTER ACCORDING TO THE NUMBER SHOWN ON THE DICE YOU THROW. YOU MUST OBEY THE INSTRUCTIONS SHOWN ON THE SQUARES YOU LAND ON. TO REACH THE 'PLANET' SQUARE YOU **MUST** THROW THE EXACT NUMBER NECESSARY. ANYTHING ELSE DOESN'T COUNT. AND IT'S THE SAME FOR LANDING BACK ON MOONBASE. NOW BLAST OFF – AND COMMANDER KOENIG GIVES YOU HIS BEST WISHES FOR A SAFE RETURN!

SPACEPROBE!

Dark are the mysteries of outer space! The planets of which we - ordinary people - have no knowledge! Worlds of monsters, and of terror! Yet there are facts, and here's your chance to see how many of them you know. Answer the questions below and check your results on page 61!

1. In our own solar system, there are nine major planets, not counting their moons. Can you give their names, without looking up a reference book?

2. Apart from those planets, there lie, between the orbits of two of them, an estimated 30,000 minor planets, or asteroids. Can you name just *one* of them?

3. The largest red star measured is Epsilon Aurigae Beta, with a diameter of 2,500 million miles. Would it be correct to say that our whole solar system could be contained within its girth?

4. How many moons has the planet Jupiter? Has it (a) 5, (b) 8, or (c) 12?

5. Of the gases to be found in planetary atmospheres, which of these found singly would be poisonous to life as we know it? Methane, Ammonia, Oxygen, Nitrogen.

6. Still on gases, if the presence of water was determined on a planet, which two gases would therefore be certain to be present?

7. The planet Mercury was named after a Roman god . . . The Messenger. What was his name in Greek mythology? (Bonus – the answer gives you a chance in question 2!)

8. Is a Super Nova (a) a newly discovered star, (b) the explosion of a distant sun, or (c) a comet passing within view of Earth?

9. Is the Milky Way (a) a galaxy, (b) a stream of space-dust within the solar system, or (c) an effect of dust particles in our upper atmosphere?

10. The first object to reach another planet from Earth was the Soviet Venus III. Did it land (a) in 1955, (b) in 1966 or (c) in 1969?

Chief Medical Officer, Moonbase Alpha -

DOCTOR HELENA RUSSELL

ONE MAN'S MEAT...

"Hallam and Whitney reporting, Commander! We're entering Area Three now!" The two space-suited men from Alpha's technological section eased their moon buggy to a halt, and began to take preliminary readings from the instruments they carried.

"Radiation level sixty above normal. Surface tremors show slight increase to point zero zero five above nil stability."

In Main Mission, Commander John Koenig sat at his desk and kept contact on an audio monitor. He glanced across at David Kano. "Got those figures?" Kano gave the thumbs-up, and Koenig said: "Okay, we copy. Go forward to the dump. But take it easy!"

Sandra Benes sat facing him, slowly running her fingers through her short, black hair. She looked worried. "What d'you think's causing it, Commander?"

Koenig shrugged. "Maybe Hallam and Whitney will tell us. Perhaps it was the narrow miss that meteorite gave us. Could have exerted some kind of magnetic pull on the covers of the nuclear waste chutes."

"That shouldn't give us too much trouble," said Tony Verdeschi. "But if they are adrift, we'd best get them secured again – real fast!" Like everyone else on Alpha, he remembered the terrifying eruption of similar chutes – deep pits of radioactive waste – that had originally caused the Moon's blast-out from Earth's orbit!

Now Kano was speaking. "That meteorite, sir. When it passed us, it failed to register again on the scanners. It might have hit us . . . "

"On the blind side where the chutes are? Maybe. Maybe that's the problem." Koenig drummed his fingers restlessly. "I suppose I should have sent up a survey Eagle at the time, just to check." He grinned lamely. "It didn't seem that important somehow!"

There was another crackle from his audio monitor, and he had to switch up the volume. Radioactivity was obviously interfering with the signals from Hallam and Whitney.

"Commander! I don't know what to make of it . . . but I think I can see something *moving* down there in the disposal area!"

"Moving?" Koenig was on his feet now. "Hallam – what the blazes do you mean, moving?"

"My stars! I can't believe it! I . . ." The gritty transmission came to an abrupt end – but not before everyone in Main Mission had heard the first split second of a desperate, panic-stricken scream!

"Eagle Three to launch station! Fully armed!" Koenig was already half way to the exit as he barked the order into his comlock. "Alan! With me!"

Together, the Commander and Alan Carter, his number one pilot, raced to the travel tube. Seconds later they were suiting up at the entry port of launch pad three, and seconds after that, their Eagle was airborne, turning its beak to the horizon, beyond which lay . . . what?

At such low level, and with radiation rife, they could maintain no visual contact with Main Mission once they were on the 'blind' side of the Moon. But the audio channels were locked open, so that Verdes-

chi and the others could hear every breath they drew.

"Should be in sight any moment now, Commander," said Carter, tersely. "Any theories?"

"Aliens. Must be. What else would explain the *movement* Hallam saw? Yes – and that was no meteorite we logged, Alan. It looked like one – but it must have been some kind of spacecraft!"

Both Koenig and Carter were prepared for a shock. What they got was far beyond even their wildest expectations. Aliens there were – just six of them. But aliens like monsters from some dreadful nightmare!

"My oath!" Carter's voice was shaking. "They – they're horrible!"

Koenig fought to control his own revulsion. He pointed through the screens of the Eagle's beak. "There are Hallam and Whitney. Looks to me like they're unharmed." The moon buggy had slewed, and its occupants were slumped in loose, unconscious poses. The aliens – the monsters – had surrounded them, but had apparently made no hostile move.

One of the hideous, coagulated faces turned slowly upwards to fix them with a wide, unblinking stare as Koenig and Carter switched to hover and sank gently down.

"You – you're not just gonna open up, Commander?" whispered the chief pilot.

Koenig just had time to shake his head before the alien spoke. At least, that was how it seemed. There was nothing in the way of radio transmission, and no sound could have carried in the airless void. It was as though his voice, projected by telepathic means, invaded their minds. And from the gasps that came from the audio monitor, Koenig knew that the people in Main Mission could hear it, too.

"We thought this place to be uninhabited. We seem to be guilty of trespass."

Koenig spoke aloud, and the alien must have received his thought patterns.

"Who are you? Where do you come from?"

"We are Lamnians, from the planet Lamnos. We are explorers, dedicated to the welfare of our people."

Koenig licked his lips. They were sand-dry. "What do you mean – welfare?"

The aliens had gathered in a body facing up at the Eagle. Alan shuddered and looked away at Hallam and Whitney. To his relief, he saw them stir as they began to come out of their totally understandable dead faint.

"Welfare?" The alien leader echoed Koenig's question. "Survival, then. We feed upon the materials you have apparently stockpiled here. Upon nuclear waste. Unfortunately, our stocks are low. Our scanners detected the presence of it on this sphere. Hence our presence. I am sorry," he added, "that we were considering stealing it. I suppose you have need of it yourselves."

"No." Koenig shook his head, inwardly thinking that the alien didn't sound as sorry as he made out. "It is useless to us. Indeed, in certain circumstances, it can be a positive danger. Like now. I must insist that you replace the chute covers you've disturbed."

There was only a moment's hesitation. Then . . . "With pleasure. And I feel this calls for a conference. I am Borg, incidentally. And you . . ?"

"Commander John Koenig. But listen, Borg. You can't possibly approach our headquarters here! You must be of a completely different metabolism. You must be so radioactive that you'd destroy us within seconds!"

"You shouldn't have told him that, Commander," said Carter. "Or maybe, you should've added that we've got lasers that could atomise him and his

chums in equal time."

They had the impression that the shapeless, monstrous lump of matter that was Borg shrugged. It must have been an impression conveyed by telepathy. "We can control our radioactivity, Commander. After all, it sustains our very existence. We do not run around spraying it hither and thither. It would be like you opening your veins and releasing your blood. How long do you think you would last?"

"He's into our minds, all right," muttered Koenig. "He's even fathomed out how we work. Alan - give her thrust and back off out of the immediate radiation zone. I want to make a test."

As Alan moved the controls to obey the order, Borg's voice came through again. "I see your wish, Commander. My people and I will follow, so that you can turn your radiation detectors full upon us. And your men . . ." he gestured to Hallam and Whitney. "Shall I convey to them your order to return to base?"

"I'll do it myself, Borg, thank you. They've had enough shocks for one day." Direct transmission put the Commander in touch with his shaken men. "Pull out. Full decontamination procedure, and check in with Doctor Russell. Then hit the sack - you've earned a break."

Borg had apparently been telling the truth. A short range check outside the radiation area proved that the aliens themselves emitted no kind of dangerous force. And they had been careful to replace the chute seals, as Koenig had asked.

"It's difficult to believe that creatures like that could be on the level," said Carter. "But I guess you just can't judge by appearances."

"Maybe not. But I'm putting full security alert on Main Mission when we let 'em in."

The impact on Koenig's colleagues was predictable to say the least. The Lamnians entered quietly, but even though they'd been warned what to expect, many of the control personnel gave way to nerves. Even the stalwart Maya had to fight panic at the sight of these beings.

So the conference was edgy. Borg and Koenig dominated it, and all eyes were on them alone. It was Borg's suggestion that, since they properly understood the dangers, Alphans should empty the chutes of nuclear waste. They – the Lamnians – would see to the loading of their ship – which was indeed the rocklike monstrosity that had appeared as a meteorite.

"You don't want the stuff, and we do. What could be simpler, Commander?" said the alien leader. "Of course, we should like to do something for you in return . . ."

"Taking our waste will be enough, Borg. I suggest we begin the operation at once. I will deploy two Eagles with grab equipment, and all available moon-buggies to assist."

"That is splendid, John Koenig." Borg snapped his baleful eyes at his followers, and they herded close together to leave Main Mission. "Come. We shall leave by the surface airlock we entered, and leave our worthy friend to make *his* preparations."

It was as they passed out to the rocky wastes beyond the Alphan complex and took the buggies that had been provided for their journey, that Maya gripped Koenig by the arm. "John! There were six of them . . . weren't there . . ?"

"Yes, Maya! *Why*?"

"Because only *five* left here! They were grouped close together – it was hard to tell. But I'm *sure* there were only five!"

With absolute certainty, Koenig knew he'd been tricked. And if one of Borg's men *had* remained within Moonbase, there was only one place he could have gone without raising the alarm. The one area where security men were never left on guard. The danger zone surrounding the reactors – vital life-core of the whole Alphan complex!

"My stars!" Koenig was ashen. "They want their nuclear waste, all right! They're going to brew up the reactors and turn the whole of Moonbase into one glorious pile of it!"

As he scrambled into a protective suit, the Commander gave his orders. Two remotely controlled Eagles, both armed with lasers, lifted to their pads and rose on their vertical ram-jets. Their targets – the moon buggies that Borg and four of his companions were even now racing back towards the dump-chute area.

Koenig himself sped to the reactor centre. Alone. He knew he'd find the outer safety door open, that his wrist-counter would register radiation already dangerously high. But with supreme disregard for his own safety, the Commander hurled his weight against the door and slammed it shut. He caught one glimpse of the missing Lamnian inside . . .

Koenig knew he'd have to go for decontamination – but there was no time for that. Not yet.

"Main Mission! Close down reactors. At once!" He spoke grimly into his comlock . . .

"But Commander! We'll lose temperature! We'll freeze within an hour!"

"So will Borg's man – and unless he does, we're doomed anyway! *Do as I say*!" Koenig switched off. He muttered, to himself . . . "Come to think of it, it'll mean the decontamination unit won't be working, either . . ."

One hour and ten minutes had passed. Thin ice had formed on the interior walls of every Moonbase building. Half dead with the numbing cold, the inhabitants were huddled together, wrapped in every available scrap of covering. Tony Verdeschi eased his cramped muscles and tottered to the switches controlling the reactors. Shakily, he thrust them back to the 'on' position . . .

Inside the reactor chambers, the lifeless lump of matter that had once been a Lamnian did not stir . . .

Slowly, warmth and life came back to the Alphans. Koenig lay unconscious in the decontamination unit, and though it would be touch and go, Helena knew that she could save him. When he did recover, she herself would have the pleasure of telling him that Borg and the others had never reached their ship. That the rocky lump they'd all thought to be a meteorite would remain on the blind side of the Moon for ever – a monument to alien treachery . . .

CLUEPIX ALPHA!

Study the pictures on this and the following two pages and solve the clues printed beneath each of them. The answers are all contained somewhere in this annual – and you'll find them together, of course, when you come to check your results on page 61!

A. Commander John Koenig is about to be savaged by a particularly hostile alien! Could he use the device seen on his belt to protect himself?

B. An Eagle is about to land on part of the Moonbase Alpha complex – or is it? How would you know for sure that this is only a model mock-up for training Eagle pilots?

C. This Eagle lifts off to combat an alien ship that menaces the Moon. It carries pilot and co-pilot – but what is the term for the frontal portion in which they sit?

D. Main Mission, Moonbase Alpha. What is the name of the girl standing, towards the left of the picture, wearing the uniform with the yellow sleeve?

E. David Kano – apparently facing an unexpected enemy! What is Kano's normal job on Alpha?

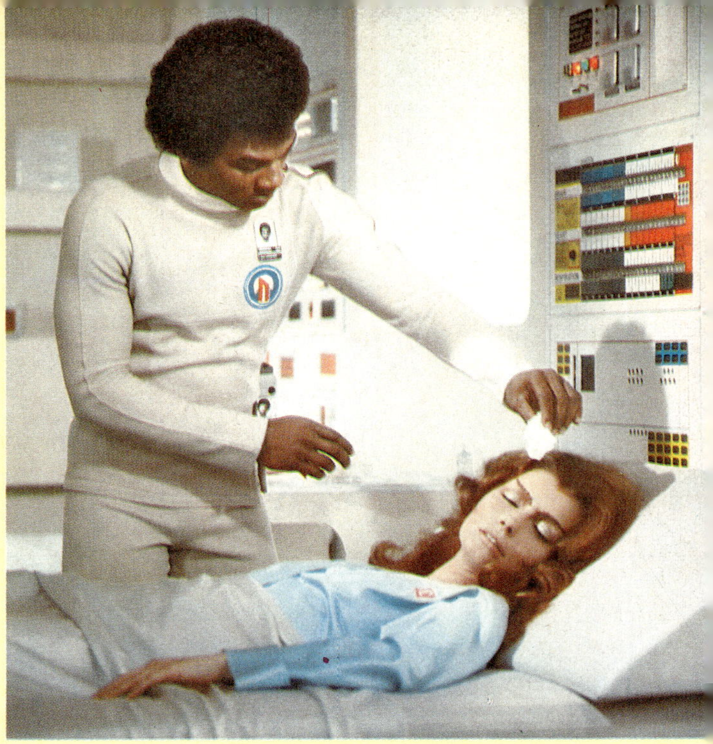

F. It's unusual to see Maya in need of hospital treatment! The man attending her is Doctor Helena Russell's assistant. What is his name?

? ? ? ? Answers

G. It's that lady from question D again – but who's she with? Give his name and his job.

H. Well, well – here he is again! Is he about to have a shave . . . or what? Put a name to the instrument he's holding in his hand.

J. Right in the hub of Moonbase Alpha, and Koenig is in touch with a survey Eagle. When passing messages, what is the phrase he uses when he asks the pilot to confirm them?

K. A serious moment for the Commander and Controller Tony Verdeschi. Name the *former* Controller whose place Tony took.

? ? ? ?
Page 61

L. Maya joined the Alpha team after the total destruction of her home planet and the death of her father. Name him, *and* name the planet.

M. Helena Russell goes glam! But what is the colour of her uniform sleeve, in keeping with her job?

FOCUS ON TONY!

It happened after the tragic space death of Paul Morrow, the original Main Mission Controller on Moonbase Alpha. There was only one possible man capable of filling Paul's place, and that was Tony Verdeschi. Of Italian origin, Verdeschi was tough. Capable. Articulate. With a highly scientific brain.

In the international world of Space 1999 characters, Tony Anholt – the man who plays Verdeschi – is himself the most international of them all. He is British, but with French, Dutch, Swedish and Irish blood.

Two series in particular have attracted attention to Tony. He was with Robert Vaughn and Nyree Dawn Porter in 'The Protectors' and portrayed the dashing young Eduard Strauss in 'The Strauss Family'. Additionally, he was seen in 'Napoleon And Love', and has guested in such popular shows as 'Jason King', 'A Family At War' and 'The Seasons'.

Son of an insurance company representative, Tony Anholt was born in Singapore in 1941, but was hurriedly evacuated to Australia, then South Africa, when the Japanese arrived.

His travels continued. He was taken to Burma, then London, where he went to school. His working life began – would you believe – as a tea-taster, but he left to join an uncle in selling toys, dolls and fancy goods. After that, he was teaching English and Latin at a school in Herne Bay.

His rolling stone way of life didn't stop there! He joined an insurance company, left it to return to teaching, and in fact taught English in Barcelona. A spell with a travel company took him to Paris, and then he came back to Britain, where he joined a firm of publishers.

Finally – and he was still only twenty-three by this time – he took a crash course in acting, working as a night-watchman to help his expenses. He made his television debut in a potato crisps commercial!

There followed other commercials, then stage repertory, small parts in television plays and series, more stage work and his London theatre debut in 'Boys In The Band'. Spotted by Gerry Anderson, he got his first big break in Anderson's 'Protectors' series.

So Tony's stopped his wandering at last. He leaves the roaming to the *other* Tony. Verdeschi. And who can tell how far Moonbase is going to take *him!*

Tony Anholt, pictured here with Catherine Schell. Moonfact: Verdeschi's sort of sweet on Maya!

THE BEAST OF BOKASSA!

The planet they'd picked up on the Main Mission video screen had gradually drawn nearer and nearer. Until Kano's computer had officially announced that it was within range.

"Report. Gravity as Earth's. Atmosphere reveals oxygen in small quantity. Temperature low, vegetation nil!"

They had tried direct radio contact, to no effect, and Koenig had ordered the launch of a close survey Eagle. It was piloted by Alan Carter, with Tony Verdeschi and Helena Russell as supernumeraries.

Now the Eagle had landed on the barren, inhospitable terrain, and Alan, Tony and Helena had emerged onto the surface, still suited up to make spot checks on the breathable quality of the thin air around them.

It was Alan Carter who caught the sudden flicker of reflected movement in the glass face-shield of his helmet. He spun round, and his yell of warning over the inbuilt communication system brought his companions whirling round in alarm!

"Ye gods! *Look*!"

Staring at them from the lip of a rocky ridge not twenty yards away was a creature – a gigantic thing more than eight feet tall. A terrifying beast with a scaled, reptilian face, its body covered in matted, shaggy hair!

They stood frozen . . . but not for long! The beast shambled down towards them, its enormous feet scattering rocks and dust, and Tony Verdeschi swung up his stun-gun!

"No! *Wait*!" Helena's cry came too late – for a blasting lance of energy shot from the gun-barrel to catch the beast low on the left arm! There was a screeching yell that they heard even through their helmets, and then the massive creature turned

and scrambled away over the ridge, to disappear from their sight!

"Didn't you sense it?" Helena turned on Tony in fury. "It had intelligence! It tried to communicate just before you fired! There were *thought*-waves!"

"*I* didn't feel them, Helena. And better to be safe than sorry. Anyhow . . . it's gone."

Even as Tony finished speaking, there came a soft rushing through the air – inaudible to them. But a chunk of rock twice the size of a football struck him fairly and squarely in the chest, and before the horrified eyes of his friends he pitched backwards, crashed to the ground, rolled over . . . and lay ominously still!

They were still crouched over his fallen body when the voice came.

"Stand up. Try nothing . . . and keep perfectly still!"

Slowly, they straightened, and then strong, scaly fists gripped their arms, choking cries from them as they spun them round. What they saw brought their hearts leaping into their mouths – for if the beast had been horrendous, this newcomer was *doubly* so! A bovine face . . . massive, upthrust horns . . . a single, glittering eye set centrally in its forehead. Like a devil, drawn by some half-crazed mediaeval artist!

"Who are you? And why did you attack my servant?" The voice was shrill and metallic, even though they instinctively knew that they only understood by some telepathic means.

"I ask you again! *Who*?"

Alan Carter found his voice. "We are space travellers. We come from a planet called Earth. We had hoped that this place might provide us with a new home . . ."

"Which it won't," muttered Helena. "The oxygen just isn't sufficient . . ."

Their captor didn't relax his grip. Forcibly – and his grasp on them was so strong that they were unable to struggle – he steered them towards a high bank of rocks in which they could make out the shape of a cave-mouth.

"Look – we didn't mean to harm your servant. Can't you realise how it looked to us? He was – monstrous. Frightening. And Tony thought *he* was going to attack!"

"It is of no matter. Perhaps he will return. Perhaps not. In the meantime, you will take his place!"

Helena turned her head back towards Tony Verdeschi's prostrate form. "Wait! What – what about *him* . . ?"

"He is dead. He is of no possible use, either to me or to you. Now – keep silent while I conduct you down to *my* domain! You are the captives of Bokassa the scientist – and fitting subjects for my experiments!"

In Main Mission, Moonbase Alpha, Commander John Koenig sat relaxed at his desk. On the big video screen, the image of the planet.

Sandra Benes walked across to join him. "It's been some time since we've had any contact from Doctor Russell and the others, sir . . ."

"They'll get in touch in good time, Sandra. We don't have them tied to our apron strings, you know. I dare say they're making as full a survey as possible before they report." Koenig glanced across at Maya. "Pull up a close picture on video, will you?"

The scene on the screen enlarged. To show the landed Eagle. Undamaged. Unharmed. And all around it the clutter of rocks, the ridges, rifts and canyons that made up the planet's surface. Oddly – though of course it didn't seem odd to Koenig and his colleagues – there was no sprawled figure where Tony Verdeschi had fallen . . .

Koenig said: "They're probably hunting around in some caves somewhere. Clearly, there's no life of any sort on the surface, but there may be greater warmth in the interior."

"I can't say I fancy the idea of taking up the life of a cave-dweller, John," smiled Maya. "No matter how cosy it is. I think I'd rather stay here and take my chances."

"Me too," confessed the Commander. "But let's not jump to any conclusions before we hear from them, huh?"

He sat back, totally at ease. It was lucky for his

peace of mind that he couldn't have actually seen beneath the surface of that planet . . . to the dismal, phosphorescent cavern where Alan Carter and Helena Russell, divested of their space-suits, hung like criminals endungeoned by some ancient king, their wrists above them, shackled to iron ring-bolts in the rocky wall!

Tony Verdeschi was far from being as dead as Bokassa had imagined. He'd slowly come back to consciousness, to find himself alone. And groggily, he'd neglected to return to the Eagle and inform Moonbase of the situation. It was perhaps a foolish oversight, but a man in a dazed condition, faced with the disappearance of his friends, does not always act rationally.

He cast about him, looking for tracks on the gritty ground . . . but there were none. The very nature of the terrain refused to show much in the way of marks.

Dizzily, he wandered towards the rocky wall beyond him, with its cave-mouth openings. "Surely – surely they wouldn't just have *left* me . . ?"

Then he heard it. A distant scrabbling sound, from somewhere deep within one of the shafts. Gingerly, he lowered himself inside, and found his boots met a gentle slope. Around him, the rocks glowed with their own phosphorescence, lighting his way. Automatically, he checked his wrist counter for radiation. There was none. He went deeper, dropping, he estimated, some two feet with every ten he traversed. It was steep. And it was becoming unbearably sticky in his suit. The external temperature must be rising.

Again, he checked, and on impulse, shed the restricting clothing, piling it in a heap against the tunnel wall. The air was breathable, though he had to take great gulps of it to power his flagging muscles. Prudently, he kept his stun-gun ready in his right fist . . .

Abruptly, as he negotiated the twists and turns of the tunnel, Tony came to the door. It was of sheer sheet metal, and it barred his way. He could still hear the scrabbling . . . but it came from beyond the barrier.

"Dare nothing – win nothing!" The strange quotative thought flashed through his mind as he pointed his gun and fired. And the metal buckled and ripped under the power of the laser blast!

He was ready for immediate action, but the smooth emptiness of the cylindrical metal passageway yawned derisively back at him.

And then, from a corner, it appeared! The beast! The very beast he'd shot in the moment of arrival on the planet!

Tony raised his gun at arm's length – but he never drew trigger! The beast was lurching drunkenly, its left arm hanging useless, its right outstretched as if in supplication. And now he caught what Helena had said . . . the tingle of telepathic transmission from the reptilian face with its wide, sad eyes . . .

"Spare me! Spare me! I – need – *help*!"

Then, slowly, the beast toppled headlong, and lay prone at Tony's feet!

The humanitarian instincts of Tony Verdeschi's mind dictated his reaction. His keen brain dictated his response. Swiftly, he bent over the fallen beast and examined the torn, bleeding left arm. Cautious pressure told him that the bone structure was humanoid. And that the upper arm was broken. He looked about him, and two swift laser-shots broke off flat metal stanchions that he could use as splints. With his own shirt, ripped to strips, he staunched the beast's wound, strapped up the arm. Then he stood up and stepped back, for the frog-like eyes had flickered.

"Thank you . . . thank you! I feared you would kill me!"

"I meant to. Before. But I thought . . ."

"Yes. Yes. I know I must be horrific to your eyes. Indeed – I mean no insult – *you* are just as repulsive to me!" The beast rose carefully, his left shoulder sagging as if to keep all effort from his injured limb.

"I have no name to give you," he said. "Bokassa allowed me nothing. Not even that."

"Bokassa . . ?"

"I saw him strike you down. And seize your companions. He is evil. The most evil of the race of devils who rule this planet. *So* evil, in fact, that they banished him to this region."

"You're speaking in riddles, my friend . . ." Tony reached out to give the beast support as he staggered weakly. It wasn't easy. The creature must have weighed half a ton.

"Bokassa is a black scientist. A master of unspeakable arts! He took me from the slave race that inhabits a distant continent. Brought me here. And gave me intelligence, and power. He sought to make me a fiend – a monster to turn loose on his own kind. But I rebelled. That very intelligence he implanted in my poor mind told me that to serve him would be wrong. Terribly wrong!"

Tony whitened. "And – and you had *escaped* from him when I cut you down . . ?"

The beast nodded. "I did not know who you were, or where you came from. But I sensed compassion. I was going to turn to you for aid . . ."

There was nothing Tony could say. He couldn't meet those eyes. Disgusted with his own impulsive instincts, he thrust the stun-gun into his belt. But the beast restrained him.

"No! You – *we* will need that. Bokassa has your friends prisoner. We must rescue them before he turns his ghastly experiments upon *their* bodies! And if he catches us, you must be ready to shoot – and this time, shoot to kill!"

Gone was any sense of relaxation in Main Mission. It *had* been too long since the last contact. John Koenig knew that something *must* have happened to his survey team.

"Kano. I'm leaving you in charge. I'm going down there myself, with an armed Eagle."

"I'm coming with you, John." This was Maya.

There was no time to argue. Curtly, the Commander nodded, and the two of them suited up and took the travel tube to launch-bay six . . .

Meanwhile, on the planet, Tony and the beast had reached their objective. It had taken all Tony's frantic gestures to stop Helena and Alan crying out in relief as they came into view. And mercifully, Bokassa had not yet come to call for them. The vile scientist was apparently not yet ready for them!

"Alan! Helena! Don't be alarmed! He's on our side!" Tony gave them the whole story as the beast himself used his mammoth strength to snap the shackles.

"I know the way! Quickly! Before Bokassa comes!" The beast led them at a dead run back through the tunnels.

"Our suits! Bokassa has them!" gasped Helena.

"No matter! The outside temperature will not harm you in the short time it will take to reach your craft!"

"You're coming with us!" Tony Verdeschi panted the words, his breath rasping in the oxygen-starved air. "We're not leaving you behind after what you've done!"

"Merely be concerned with Bokassa," said the beast. "His strength is even more than mine! And if he detects us, his cunning is such that we may none of us be going anywhere – save to our doom!"

But Bokassa was not after them. As far as he was concerned, Tony was dead, his beast had fled, and his captives were still where he had imprisoned them. No – *his* attention had focussed on the new threat from the skies. The Eagle bearing John Koenig and Maya to his domain!

His single eye blazing with fury, he crouched behind the rocks, even as the Eagle landed. He remained perfectly still as the two occupants got out, walked warily across the dirt-strewn ground. And then he struck!

His savage yell brought Koenig and Maya spinning round – but then he was on them! One steel-like hand grabbed Maya and flung her headlong, his other fist sending Koenig sprawling in a headlong tangle! His bellows of rage struck fear into them as, the wan light glinting on his massive horns, he lifted his huge feet for the crushing death-blow!

And then it happened! The onrush of the scaly-headed reptilian with the matted body-hair. So far ahead of his gasping companions with their air-hungry lungs. The onset of the beast with nothing but the lust for vengeance in his tortured soul. That, and the feeling of comradeship for these people whose one representative had been the only living being ever to show him compassion . . .

Locked together, beast and master staggered in shuffling deadlock over the rocks. The beast's hands were locked round Bokassa's throat!

"Come on! We've got to get out of here!" Alan Carter rasped out the words, hauling Koenig and Maya to their feet. "We can't stay! We *can't* !"

Numbly, they let themselves be shoved towards their Eagle. But Helena was struggling with Tony Verdeschi, their conflict almost mirroring the giant battle between Bokassa and his beast . . .

"Let me go, Helena! Let me go! We've *got* to bring him along!"

"No, Tony! No! Don't you see? How could *he* exist with us on Alpha? This is his place – and this is his destiny!"

Desperately, Helena summoned up the last reserves of her waning strength and drove a round-house right fist to the point of Tony's jaw . . .

The savage planet was far behind them now. The Moon was almost beyond reach of it. In Main Mission, Commander Koenig sat behind his usual desk, and Maya, Helena and Alan Carter were near him. There was a gloomy silence there, and all eyes were on Tony Verdeschi, who was immobile, his hands clasped before him, staring up at the waning picture of Bokassa's sphere on the big video screen.

"A beast. And yet a beast with honour. A mind worthy of taking its place alongside any of us." Verdeschi sounded bitter. Then he turned and shrugged. "But I suppose that very mind *was* the product of Bokassa's own researches . . ."

Koenig stood up and walked across to him, placing his hand on his controller's shoulder. "Exactly, Tony. Do you remember the old story of a Professor Frankenstein, who created a monster that, in the end, destroyed him? It's the same with your beast. And if he won the struggle, perhaps he can use his intelligence, somehow, to make that planet a better place. All we can be sure of is that it wasn't the place for *us* . . ."

CHALLENGE!
MY OATH! THIS COULD BE OUR NEW HOME! TRY RADIO CONTACT, SANDRA...
ATMOSPHERE-COMPATIBLE! GRAVITY AS EARTH! SPECTROSCOPE RECORDS VEGETATION...
A BLANKET TRANSMISSION GOES OUT...
NO, GARRAK. DO NOT ANSWER. NOT YET. LET US WAIT...
A PLANET INTO WHOSE AREA THE WAYWARD MOON HAS DRIFTED ON ITS ENDLESS JOURNEY THROUGH SPACE...
NOTHING, COMMANDER...
VERY WELL. MAYA, ALAN AND I WILL TAKE AN EAGLE AND GO DOWN FOR A CLOSER RECONNAISSANCE...
THEN SUDDENLY...
STOP, KOENIG! YOU COMMIT THE CRIME OF TRESPASS!
WHAT THE BLAZES..? WHO ARE YOU? HOW DO YOU KNOW MY NAME?
KARKK KNOWS EVERYTHING! WE HAVE SEEN YOUR APPROACH, KOENIG - AND WE KNOW WHAT YOU WANT!
YOU WILL MAKE NO ATTEMPT TO LAND ON THE PLANET JARKAN!
JARKAN. YOUR PLANET?
NOT YET. AS FAR AS WE KNOW, IT IS UNINHABITED. BUT WE, TOO, ARE SEEKING A NEW WORLD FOR OUR PEOPLES - AND JARKAN IS IDEAL!

IT SEEMS WE HAVE A PROBLEM. A CASE OF 'I WAS HERE FIRST.' DO YOU THINK WE SHOULD BOW TO THE WILL OF THIS – KARKK..?
DON'T BE DICTATED TO, COMMANDER! WHO'S HE TO ISSUE ORDERS?
NO WAY! WHO DOES HE THINK HE IS?
THE VIDEO SCREEN BLANKED FOR A MOMENT. THEN...
LOOK COMMANDER! LOOK WELL! THIS IS MY SHIP. A COLONY OF MORE THAN SIX HUNDRED BEINGS. AND FULLY–I REPEAT–FULLY ARMED!
KOENIG IS IMPRESSED. HE'D BE LESS THAN HUMAN OTHERWISE...
VERY WELL, KARKK. I TAKE IT YOU ARE FUGITIVES FROM SOME DESTROYED PLANET..? YOU ARE IN A SIMILAR SITUATION TO US. CAN WE TALK?
SIRE, SIRE!
TALK? TALK? WHO DOES THIS FOOL THINK HE IS! NOBODY QUESTIONS KARKK'S WISHES! NOBODY!
CALM YOURSELF. THIS KOENIG HAS SPIRIT! ONLY CUNNING WILL OVERCOME HIM!
MAYBE YOU'RE RIGHT! YES. I SHALL BE CAUTIOUS. TOO MUCH IS AT STAKE...

AN EAGLE LEAVES MOONBASE ALPHA...
I DON'T LIKE THIS, COMMANDER! NOT ONE LITTLE BIT.
RELAX, ALAN. WE'RE ARMED, AREN'T WE? AND KARKK IS COMING OUT IN A SHUTTLE TO MEET US MIDWAY...
HE'S STILL ABOUT THE MOST UNTRUSTWORTHY BLOKE I'VE EVER CLAPPED EYES ON!
YOU WORRY TOO MUCH. COULD BE WE'LL COME TO SOME AGREEMENT ABOUT THIS PLANET, JARKAN...
SHOULD WE NOT MAKE OUR PRESENCE KNOWN, MORROK?
WAIT, MY SON. HAVE **PATIENCE...** WE MUST SEE MORE OF THESE ALIENS!
WELL, KARKK?
YES. I AM WELL. BUT NO MATTER. I HAVE CAST OFF MY SHUTTLE FERRY. SHALL WE GO FORWARD, SO THAT YOU CAN SEE WHAT HAPPENS TO IT?
IRRITATED, BUT INTRIGUED, KOENIG AGREES...
WATCH, COMMANDER. MY OWN SHIP IS NOT IN DIRECT VIEW, BUT I LEFT MY ORDERS...

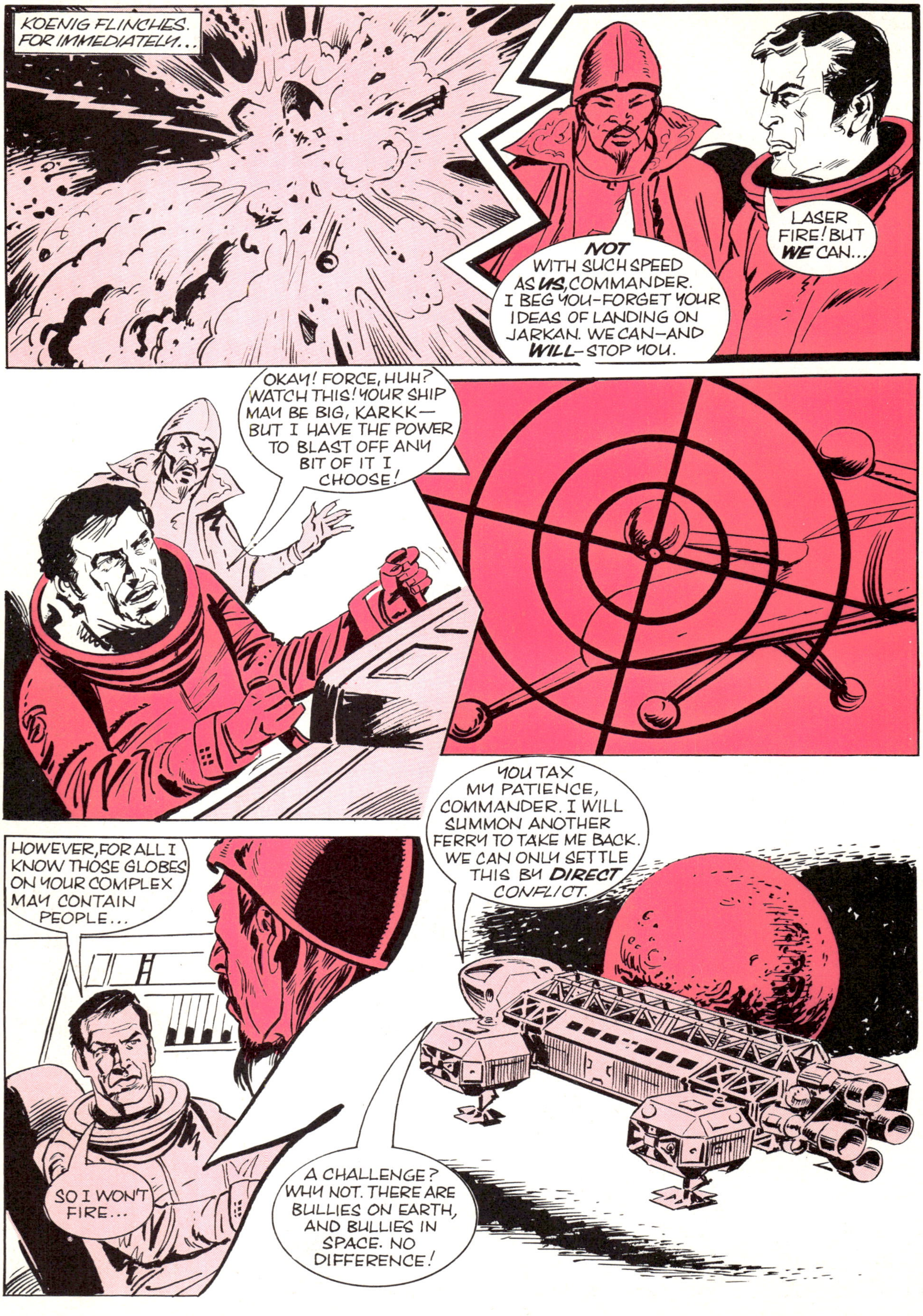
KOENIG FLINCHES. FOR IMMEDIATELY...
LASER FIRE! BUT WE CAN...
NOT WITH SUCH SPEED AS US, COMMANDER. I BEG YOU-FORGET YOUR IDEAS OF LANDING ON JARKAN. WE CAN-AND WILL-STOP YOU.
OKAY! FORCE, HUH? WATCH THIS! YOUR SHIP MAY BE BIG, KARKK—BUT I HAVE THE POWER TO BLAST OFF ANY BIT OF IT I CHOOSE!
HOWEVER, FOR ALL I KNOW THOSE GLOBES ON YOUR COMPLEX MAY CONTAIN PEOPLE...
SO I WON'T FIRE...
YOU TAX MY PATIENCE, COMMANDER. I WILL SUMMON ANOTHER FERRY TO TAKE ME BACK. WE CAN ONLY SETTLE THIS BY DIRECT CONFLICT.
A CHALLENGE? WHY NOT. THERE ARE BULLIES ON EARTH, AND BULLIES IN SPACE. NO DIFFERENCE!

WHAT DO YOU THINK, MORROK?
THE SAME AS YOU, PROBABLY. WHAT ENSUES WILL BE MOST INTERESTING! TAKE CARE TO TRANSMIT NOTHING. NEITHER OF THEM MUST KNOW OF OUR EXISTENCE...
KOENIG AND CARTER RETURN AT FULL SPEED...
ERECT ALL DEFENSIVE SHIELDS AS SOON AS WE'VE DOCKED! PREPARE ALL LASER BATTERIES! WE'VE GOT A FIGHT ON OUR HANDS!
THEN...
YE GODS! THE TREACHEROUS DEVIL! HE'S OPENED FIRE WITHOUT GIVING US A CHANCE TO ORGANISE!
THA-BOOOMMM!
FORCE-SHIELDS INOPERATIVE, MOONBASE ALPHA IS A SITTING DUCK!
MAIN LIGHTING GONE! VIDEO SCREEN AND TRANSCEIVERS INOPERATIVE! LASER BATTERIES ONE AND TWO KNOCKED OUT!
WE'RE NOT GOING TO SURVIVE THIS! WE'RE GOING TO BE ANNIHILATED!
KOENIG AND CARTER BATTLE TO GAIN ENTRY...
EMERGENCY DOOR'S... JAMMED...

IT IS TIME WE INTERVENED. I THINK IT IS CLEAR ENOUGH WHICH OF THESE PEOPLES WE WOULD WELCOME...
...AS COLONISTS ON OUR PLANET...
THE BETA LANCE, THEN, MORROK? AT ONCE!
A SWIFT ORDER...AND DECISIVE ACTION!
IT IS DONE. CALL JOHN KOENIG ON MOON-BASE, GARRAK. TELL HIM THAT WE WILL BE GLAD TO RECEIVE HIM AS A FRIEND. HE HAS SHOWN THE FINE QUALITIES OF MERCY AND INTEGRITY...
THEN-THE SUPREME IRONY! WITH THEIR COMMUNICATIONS SYSTEMS KNOCKED OUT, THE ALPHANS HAVE NO MEANS OF HEARING MORROK'S MESSAGE!
KARKK MUST HAVE MADE SOME KIND OF MISTAKE ...BLOWN HIMSELF UP! LUCKY FOR US. REPORT DAMAGE, KANO-ESTIMATE TIME FOR REPAIRS AND CONTROL!
THIRTY SIX HOURS AT LEAST, COMMANDER. WE'LL HAVE TO ABANDON ANY IDEA OF GOING DOWN TO LOOK AT THAT PLANET. WE'LL BE OUT OF ITS RANGE BY THEN...
AND SO THE ALPHANS ARE FATED NEVER TO KNOW HOW CLOSE THEY CAME TO FINDING A NEW AND PERFECT HOME...

SPOT THE DIFFERENCE

The pictures below are identical – or are they? In fact, the bottom picture has ten small changes. So see if you can spot them!
Answers, page 61.

CODEX COMCON!

When this alien arrives on Moonbase Alpha, normal translator/communicators are useless. This being is totally mute! He can only express himself by drawing symbols – an alphabet that the Main Mission computer has to unscramble. Below is the alien's message, and the key to the code. How fast can *you* unscramble what he wants? You won't beat the computer – but you can check your results on page 61!

Alien Message:

ABCDEFGHIJKLMNOPQRSTUVWXYZ

MOON-BEAMS

MIND THAT ASTEROID! YOU'RE GOING TOO FAST! LOOK OUT FOR THIS IDIOT ON THE MONOPOD! WATCH THOSE GYROS...

NO—**YOU** TELL HIM WE'VE COME IN PEACE...

HE SAYS WE'RE ON DOUBLE YELLOW LINES!

CALLING MISSION CONTROL! YOU'RE NOT GOING TO BELIEVE THIS, BUT WHEN WE REACHED THE MILKY WAY...

RIDICULOUS! NOTHING COULD BE AS HIDEOUS AS **THAT!**

WHAT did they say?

JUST FOR FUN, A SELECTION OF PICTURES FROM THE MOONBASE FILES WITH SOME WACKY DIALOGUE ADDED! IT WAS MAYA'S IDEA- SHE'S FULL OF MISCHIEF, THAT ONE!

I'VE ALWAYS SAID JOHN NEEDED GLASSES...

SMILE, PLEASE— YOU'RE ON CANDID CAMERA...

WHY ARE YOU FLYING UPSIDE DOWN, CARTER?
I AM AN AUSTRALIAN, AREN'T I...?

YOU PAINTED THIS LOVELY MAP OF YOUR PLANET...?
I'M NOT JUST A PRETTY FACE...

Maya's Crossword

Here's a crossword that Maya has specially set for you. Can you solve it? The answers are at the foot of the next column.

CLUES ACROSS

2. Location (as of a building).
4. Scaled down copy of an object.
8. Pinch.
9. Crossword-setter!
11. _ _ and behold!
12. Not vegetable, not mineral!
14. Bricks are fired in this.
16. Injures.
17. Opposite of win.
20. Molecule vital to human life.
21. _ _ and fro.
22. Thick form of milk.
24. Workers' alliance.
27. MAIN MISSION.
29. Capable of hearing.
30. Little.
32. Preposition of place.
33. To employ.
34. To slacken off.
36. To fetch.
38. Opposite of first.
41. Alphan Commander.
43. For example.
44. Common metal.
46. Girl's name.
47. Popular type of steam bath.
48. Name of the Thames at Oxford.

CLUES DOWN

1. Actor who plays Verdeschi.
2. Healthy watering-place.
3. Neat.
4. Of me.
5. Traditional English tree.
6. An old cloth measure.
7. Our capital city.
9. MAIN MISSION.
10. Girl's name. Also famous battle.
13. Polite term for lady.
15. Exists.
18. Mark left by a wound.
19. Great American lake.
21. Term for 100 mph.
23. Opposite of beginning.
24. United States of America.
25. Three times three.
26. Atom, or jot.
27. Found in front of a front door.
28. Theatre background.
29. Moonbase craft. (plural).
31. Doctor Russell's first name.
33. Villain in 'Planet of The Apes'.
35. You and me.
37. Daily paper animals???
39. Mohammedan leader.
40. Another name for a can.
42. Vapour.
45. Royal Artillery (abbrev.).

ANSWERS TO QUIZ AND PUZZLE PAGES

SPACEPROBE – P 32.

1. Mercury, Venus, Earth, Mars, Jupiter, Saturn, Uranus, Neptune and Pluto.
2. Ceres, Vesta and Hermes are the best known.
3. No. Only as far as Saturn.
4. Twelve moons.
5. All except for Oxygen.
6. Oxygen and Hydrogen.
7. Hermes.
8. The explosion of a distant sun.
9. A galaxy . . . ours.
10. 1966.

CLUEPIX ALPHA – Pp 39 – 41.

A. No. It is a Comlock – a communicator.
B. Apart from suspension threads, the retros are not firing!
C. Not nose, schnoz or hooter – but beak!
D. Sandra Benes.
E. In charge of computers.
F. Doctor Mathias.
G. Chief pilot Alan Carter.
H. Like in question 'A' – it's a Comlock.
J. "Do you copy?"
K. Paul Morrow.
L. Mentor, of the planet Psychon.
M. White, like all medical personnel.

CODEX COMCON – P 56.

I bring greetings from the planet Zoron and invite your leader to meet our President.

Spot The Difference, P. 19.

Shadow inside neck of spacesuit; bolt on right of spacesuit neck; extra shape above right shoulder; clip on harness; extra dot on arm-flash; broader front zipper; black line on sleeve; shorter line on front-pack; larger shadow on upper helmet; larger cuff.

Spot The Difference, P. 29.

Patterns at top left and on above-screen symbols; On screens below main one and on fire-extinguisher; Belt of right-hand man; Extra box on foreground panel; black line on screen to left of foreground woman; Extra paper on desk; black sleeve on background man.

Spot The Difference, P. 55.

Extra light; One white striplight deleted; Extra black on background panel; All white badge on Helena; Panel altered in right background; Stripes on girl's arm; Dark extra band to right of slumped man; Shadow on console beneath him; black edge behind Helena; extra white panel to left of Sandra.

ANSWERS TO CROSSWORD

ACROSS: 2. Site; 4. Model; 8. Nip; 9. Maya; 11. Lo; 12. Animal; 14. Kiln; 14. Maims; 17. Lose; 20. DNA; 21. To; 22. Cream; 24. Union; 27. Main Mission; 29. Eared; 30. Scant; 32. At; 33. Use; 34. Ease; 36. Bring; 38. Last; 41. Koenig; 43. E.G.; 44. Iron; 46. Ann; 47. Sauna; 48. Isis.

DOWN: 1. Anholt; 2. Spa; 3. Trim; 4. My; 5. Oak; 6. Ell; 7. London; 9. Main Mission; 10. Alma; 13. Madam; 15. Is; 18. Scar; 19. Erie; 21. Ton; 23. End; 24. USA; 25. Nine; 26. Iota; 27. Mat; 28. Scene; 29. Eagles; 31. Helena; 33. Urko; 35. Us; 37. Gnus; 39. Aga; 40. Tin; 42. Gas; 45. RA.

3